BRIGHT ARCHIVE

SARAH MINOR

RESCUE PRESS

CHICAGO | CLEVELAND | IOWA CITY

BRIGHT ARCHIVE

Printed in the United States of America
FIRST EDITION
ISBN 978-0-9994186-9-7

Design by Annie Leue & Sevy Perez
Americane
rescuepress.co

BRIGHT ARCHIVE

SARAH MINOR

For Liza

CONTENTS

"Wings, the mark of a bird,
are quite useless in snow."

MARY RUEFLE

THE NEW AGE /

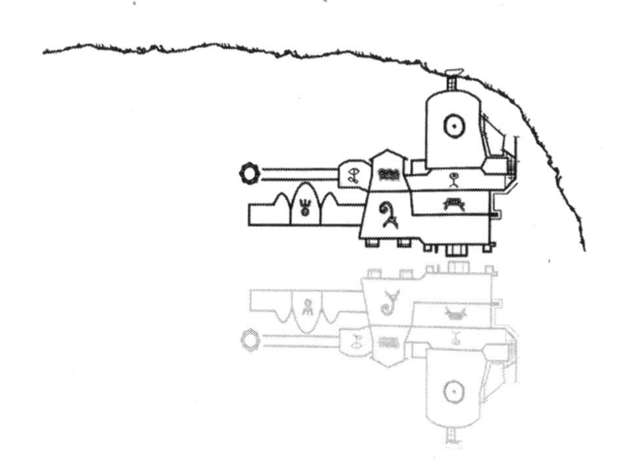

BELOW GROUND

I. ENTRANCE

The Faun holds a footrace in the southern high tunnel. It's me against the Giant and Hope the Kiwi. We go barefoot between the new furrows we spent the morning shaping under plasticine light. One hundred yams to the trough. The Faun's only rule is "don't fall."

Nate watches us from the grass past the tunnel's mouth. In high school, where we met, we sprinted for track teams that won state four years in a row and relay running got me into college. But for two months now farmers have been handing Nate the mallet and me the

---

Chiusella valley, under the daily guidance of a man named Fauno, the commune was largely unknown to English speakers but had gained relative fame in 1992 when the Italian government conducted a raid and discovered a secret underground temple the Damanhurians had been hand digging and painting for over a decade. Today the Temples of Humankind stretch three stories below ground and are advertised as "the eighth wonder of the world." Until very recently, all I could find were truncated websites, out-of-date blogs, and Italian spiritual volumes written by Airaudi. But around 2014, following the untimely death of its founder, Damanhur went fully online, accessible to the public.

nails and you could say I'm ready to prove myself in this break before lunch with the farmhands.

I'm first to the vertical sheet at the back of the tunnel but when I pivot there I slip in the new mud so hard that I fly. I feel half a yam knock against my shoulder blade where I've crushed the perfect furrow and I'm slick by the time the Giant crosses back into the grass. The Faun has turned away to face the Fairy and the Lizard by then and he's got both hands on his head, cursing in Italian.

I. ENTRANCE 

In May 2011 I finished college and my boyfriend Nate and I bought a pair of plane tickets with savings from four years working at a vet and a sandwich shop. Our plan was to spend the summer on farms across central Italy through a work-exchange called WWOOF (World Wide Organization of Organic Farms). By July we'd made it to a shadeless hill outside Florence, where each day we skinned our palms on clawed weeds growing deep in clay that made the ancient terracotta pots I'd studied in school. We shoveled and weeded in shouting distance of a British couple who liked to observe us closely while floating in a very blue, Cyprus-lined pool. It was there we signed up for the WWOOF Emergency job board and soon received an urgent email from a farm in a dire situation and at risk of losing all their crops. I replied immediately and the next day we walked three miles to a bus that took us further north, to a landscape famous for vampires. It took some time to realize where we had landed.

The Federation of Damanhur is an ecovillage and New Age community of about 1,000 followers living in a 15-kilometer property around the capital city of Damijl. In 1973 Oberto Airaudi founded the place as "a laboratory for the future of humankind." When we lived there, in the

2. THE BLUE TEMPLE

"This is the oldest hall built exclusively with hammers and chisels. This hall is available for meditations for individuals and small groups. It is also used to prepare oneself for accessing the other halls, by observing the large blue sphere."

The Walnut is our boss. He picks us up from the station at the foot of the Alps and drives us 30 kilometers out into the farm while we smile at one another a lot. Nate and I didn't do much more than pack a phrasebook for the summer, and this is the first farm where our hosts speak as little English as we do Italian.

They put us up in a three-room shed past the cow barn where the cows make themselves known from both ends at all hours. Both the lights and AC in the shed are solar powered but they only function during the day, so at sunset we lug two jugs of water across the pasture and drink from them as we sweat through the short night.

Fauno's was the only truck that could carry more than two workers. All the other vehicles were tiny one- or two-man Japanese-made cabs with short, tin flatbeds that ran off motorcycle engines. They drove like golf carts with drag and were just as likely to tip.

Every truck in Damanhur carried the same object, a nest of wires and natural stones called "selfica" technology that was our first example of the "experimental energy research" happening there. Much of Damanhur's visible spirituality had to do with directing "vital and intelligent energies," for personal and community benefit. The devices were part of what the founder, Airaudi, known in Damnahur as "Falco," claimed was an ancient tradition dating back to "Egyptian, Etruscan, Celtic and Minoan civilizations," and the items were a staple in every home. The devices on dashboards were said to funnel specific frequencies that promoted safe travel on the road the way I understand dashboard icons of St. Christopher do for modern Catholics.

Some days I sneak a slim Angela Carter paperback out to the fields by slipping it down the back of my pants so I can read under a tree when they pass around apples and crusty bread at lunch. I ration stories over the next weeks as the book blooms with a greasy stain from one cover to the next.

On the first day, the Faun drives us out to the fields. On his dashboard perches a funny wire contraption made of stones and spiraled copper. We pass corn rows, a potato patch, a fallow field, and finally spot the defunct vineyard that is ours for the afternoon. The Alps rise into the cool distance without any of the stone pines or tall cypress from the south. Flooded fields stretch in all directions with no outposts to divide them and I begin to wonder how the Nucleus manages all this space. Up close, the farmland seems to be in more trouble than they let on. Nate and I trim dead vines using pairs of small craft scissors that Faun pulls from a paper bag before leaving us. The main branches are dark and shriveled from a late frost that took the community by surprise and inspired the Faun to post on WWOOF's Emergency Board. What we know is that each cut is important. What we don't know is where the dead vine ends and the salvageable stalk remains.

2. THE BLUE TEMPLE

At first, we believed we'd arrived in a self-sufficient commune prosperous enough to support hundreds of members. Nate and I blamed our early dissonant encounters on language and cultural barriers and didn't start asking questions until the third day, when we noticed that everyone was calling each other by animal names. "Noce," the Walnut, was in fact our boss's surname. After that I started writing things down.

At first, the shed Nate and I shared seemed comical. By then we were familiar with hard labor and basic conditions, and electricity was just one among other inconsistencies on the farm. I recognize now that while our roof had a solar panel, there was no battery to store the energy it collected. But there was AC in the main house, which looked like a set of large birdhouses cobbled together to hold six families. Damanhur had 25 occupation-based "Nucleos," for farming, business, art, energy research, "mystery studies," etc., in which families pooled all income. Away from the Nucleos, all public buildings were covered in intricate eco-murals.

3. THE HALL OF WATER

"Dedicated to the feminine principle and the female divine forces, the hall of water has the shape of a chalice, a symbol of receptivity and welcoming. This hall is available for meditations on the life cycles, in preparation for childbirth, to reawaken profound memories, and to enter into contact with one's feminine essence."

On the third day we dig potatoes from a dusty field with Hope (the Kiwi) and Maria (the Spaniard) who I like automatically because they don't shave anywhere and are WWOOFers like ourselves. But Hope doesn't look at us when she speaks because, she says, of the Bush years. Maria speaks Spanish, Italian, and English but studied in Australia and says she only understands us if we speak in an Australian accent, so we speak via Hope if we can.

On the fourth day we sort a pile of potatoes as tall as the barn and glinting with hay from the eaves. The Faun has instructed us to search the harvest for blight—soft green patches that could spread to the whole stock in storage for the winter—but mostly what we do is play "rock or potato" with Hope and Maria by holding a single culprit aloft and asking for bets before throwing it hard at a wall.

At first I couldn't decide why I preferred not to work beside her. My father had sung "Summertime" to my sister and I as kids the way his mother had when he grew up in the American South. But when Silfie sang, I heard something new in her repetition of the only line she remembered, the one insisting on cotton and the seasonal harmony experienced by people who watched others work a field. I began to realize that our presence in the field brought a class consciousness to the farm workers who had left desk and teaching jobs to join the community. To be American and WWOOFing in the presence of an antebellum song so far from its context was to hear the dissonance between the work we were doing and the privilege we brought to it every day. Nate pointed out that Silfie was, like us and Gigante, one of the few very light-skinned people at Damanhur. Each time she boasted we were reincarnated from the same stock, the others turned away, and so we did too.

On the fifth day we follow the Giant outside in an attempt to avoid Hope and Maria, which is how we end up spending much of our time pulling weeds with the Lizard and the Giant, who are Argentinian and Danish, respectively.

Out in the field they teach us to grip both hands around a thick stalk and lean back using our own weight to wrench it from the ground. This is how we often end up on our backs together. Sometimes Nate links his elbows beneath my arms and we pull together and still the weeds often snap away at their base.

On the sixth day, in the fields, the Fairy stoops in long skirts and tells us about her work communicating with plants at the Mystery School in the capital. She pulls us into her arms and announces loudly, "We are ancestors." The Fairy is always singing "Summertime and the living is easy. Fish are jumping and the cotton is high," in a heavy accent, to show off her English, which we are grateful for when she explains when dinner is and where we can find fruit in the big house before we go out for the day. The deal is that we work six days a week for a bed and three meals a day but we are never offered very much to eat.

3. THE HALL OF WATER

Like other WWOOFers, Hope was working farms as a way to travel between jobs. She was studying to teach Montessori in Rome, where Montessori began. She said the language of Montessori, based on four different "planes" of development, was not unlike Damanhur's tiered structure. Silfie, who sang in long skirts, belonged to "class C," which meant that she spent only three days a week working the farm and gave only part of her income. At the time it did not occur to me to ask where else she lived. It was Silfie who first explained "the music of the plants," the experimental research in which Damanhurians performed outdoor concerts that prompted specific species to harmonize with human musicians.

4. HALL OF SPHERES

"This hall hosts nine spheres, eight of which are positioned in lateral niches. During the experience of Contact with the Cosmos, held during different times of the year, the spheres can be used for experimental research to contact non-earthly intelligences."

We don't see the Walnut often because he is head of the Nucleus and out on business for much of the day. Nate plays with the Walnut's children most evenings and it's the kids who start teaching us Italian while we eat with all 40 Nucleus members family-style at the long wooden table where people have to take turns sitting to eat. The Walnut's children keep a pet fox named Baby Fox who runs long laps among the work boots beneath the table during meals, gobbling scraps. Through hand gestures and single words the Walnut explained that Baby Fox was found drowning in a puddle in the barn during a midsummer storm. He is about the length of a cat but plays like a dog and is faster than both with sharper teeth.

Baby Fox is the first Damanhurian I truly befriend and eventually he prefers to sit in my lap at the table while I eat quickly and my knees get raw and cross-hatched beneath his paws. Nate, who works at vets at home, gives me firm looks.

The three little Noces moved everywhere with a pack of children from the Nucleo who were treated like a complex organism by two silent, unsmiling women who herded them in and out of the kitchen. Despite the evidence of regular reproduction at Damanhur, Gigante explained that the community had experienced a significant decline in population since the '70s. The "New Life" program, which had brought Gigante in, had been instituted in an unprecedented move to invite non-original or born-in members to join Damanhur.

I had surprised myself before we left to WWOOF when I asked Nate to move to Arizona with me the next fall. We had both grown up in Iowa, the first secular generation in a line of Lutherans and Baptists and Presbyterians, and this quality had set us apart from several devout peers at home. When my parents divorced in fourth grade, my mother reframed herself in new spiritual terms. She went back to grad school in Medieval History to study the economic power of farmlands owned and operated by houses of nuns. She lined her long desk with photocopies of early medieval spreadsheets and our new condominium with candles and wall-sized tapestries from museum gift shops. She put two Loreena McKennitt albums on repeat for three years. Later, it was true that when the Damanhurians described their energy devices, their plant musicals, their naming rituals, and their lives that moved with the cycles of the land, Nate stepped back, but I leaned forward.

On the seventh day the Walnut kindly explains that the family hopes we can take Baby Fox with us when we leave because he and I have grown attached. Once I communicate that all I have is a backpack and a train pass the Walnut tells me, "Think about him when you go dreaming. He tell you what he need."

On the eighth day Lizard and Giant confess that they are "Young Life" which means that their Damanhurian names aren't entirely official yet, but the Nucleus is letting the two of them test the language out to see how the intelligent energies vibe in return. Giant says they still can't participate in the annual group photo where the entire populace is photographed wearing white. We don't ask them what full membership means because usually Lizard gestures "no" at Giant whenever the big guy begins to explain something in depth. Lizard is wiry and serious and doesn't like to answer our questions. He is newer to Damanhur than the Giant and after two days with the three of us he moves to another part of the field to work alone.

Later the Giant will tell us quietly that his birth name is Johannes. We three spend the afternoon sitting in the cracked field and imagining what our Damanhurian names would be if we stuck around. "Baby Fox," says Giant, winking at me about something that seems already a joke, and I am surprised to feel pleased. "And you," he says, turning to Nate, "a healer, no, a wizard, no, a Wren. A quick bird and a bright one, like your hair."

4. HALL OF SPHERES 

I wrote down almost everything that our boss, Noce, said because it was usually a little fantastic and also very concise. He always wore the same sweater and was taller than every doorway he encountered. Nate had noticed that he moved soundlessly, like a vampire. Through a series of exchanges, Noce gradually conveyed that I had made a kind of commitment to the little fox Volpino and would hurt him if I left him behind at the end of our stay.

I've learned since that many Damanhurians studied animal communication, which I found complicated because by no means were those we sat with at the long table vegetarians. Additionally, the animals on the farm who were given names were only called by the name of their species, while humans had both an animal and a plant name chosen for them by the group through a complicated ritual. The cows and chickens did not have names, it seemed, because eventually they were to be eaten. By the end of the first week we learned from Gigante that Noce's full name was Tocchino Noce (Turkey Walnut), which matched the animal-plant structure assigned to everyone we met except for Silfie and Gigante who inexplicably had mythical creatures in place of animal names.

Noce's three children—two boys and a girl—hadn't yet reached the age when they'd be given official names and introduced themselves to us all as "Noce" though they laughed when they said it, which may have signaled a joke or play.

5. HALL OF METALS

"This is a circular temple dedicated to metals and to time. This hall is available for meditations connected to one's life path, to contact oneself in different moments in time, and to prepare for making inspired choices."

On our tenth day the Faun drives us to the capital city, Damijl, where we find our first real trouble. We are neither New Life nor paying visitors and have no credits (minted in Damijl) to our name, so it takes a cameo from the Walnut to get us in to see the founder, the Falcon Dandelion, deliver a talk on the green.

There is a lot to look at in Damijl, and more to buy. A shop at the front gate sells "selfic" devices for the mantle, the car, the headboard, the pocket, the neck, the ears, and the ankle. Every two-story wall features a collage of animals, plants and cosmic imagery at large scale and rendered in a style that seems a combination of amateur talent and sheer will. The grounds of the capitol feature labyrinths laid with painted stones in every open space. Two outdoor galleries are circled by free-standing Corinthian columns that alternate with statues of figures like Horace, Jesus, and Durga, all made of the same low-grade plaster. Every major religion is co-mingled. Nate and I are in our farm clothes. Everyone else is wearing white. To kill time, we walk a blue labyrinth. Halfway through, a woman approaches us smiling hard. She reminds us not to cross the boundary lines or we will de-energize the labyrinth for an hour. Once she's is out of sight, Nate rests his work boot on top of the stone and I glance around us quickly. Soon the Faun collects us and we join nearly a hundred people seated in folding chairs on a patch of brown grass while Falcon Dandelion speaks through a clip-on mic. The leader of Damanhur is younger and shorter than I expected and handsome in a cruel way, with a cropped beard that pours into his hair to make the stylish Italian helmet I've seen in cafés.

On the same day I discovered Damanhur's new, official online presence I came across the third most popular hit, *Damanhur Inside Out*, a WordPress site authored by people who claim to have escaped the severe mind control they were under while living in Damanhur. They cite articles from *Focus*, an Italian scientific journal naming Damanhur one of the most prominent mind-control cults in Italy. The site's main page reads: "It has made one man very wealthy and his followers exceedingly impoverished. Stripped of all their material assets, their debts increase as his wealth accumulates in Swiss bank accounts and off-shore investments. The latest scam has been to persuade all the remaining founder members of the real estate cooperative to sign away their shares in Damjjl, leaving him the sole owner of all the original houses. You certainly cannot rely on the British or American media to give you an accurate picture. Filmmakers and journalists have all been taken in by its superficial glamor, efficient marketing and completely indoctrinated PR staff. Former members are too scared to talk or give evidence and it's hard to build a legal case against the Community without it."

His voice is tight and his eyes are everywhere but even the children in the dirt sit rapt as he pac-es. Occasionally a listener will lift their eyes or hands to the sky. Someone in front of me has an earbud with English translation piped through, and I cock my head sharply to listen in. Like most sermons I've witnessed, the Falcon's talk relies on a shared context and vocabulary, but from what I gather he spends the hour explaining various modes of ascension. Afterwards, we stand and mill around and the Faun introduces us to Swan Banana and Snail Coffee, who speak English and are interested in WWOOF, an organization I suddenly realize I know very little about. Then the Faun takes us aside. He offers us a visit to the Temples of Humankind, the ones that stretch somewhere beneath us. Nate scoffs. "How much?" "40 credits," the Faun says, "for a tour of the eighth wonder of the world." Nate rolls his eyes, "That's 60 US to see a church." "We'll get back to you?" I ask louder, but the Faun turns both palms forward.

On the eleventh day when we return to the Nucleo sunburned and soiled from afternoon work, someone pulls us into the hot kitchen where the families are celebrating the birthday of Snake, the Nucleo's oldest member who is either turning 89 or 75—his age is debated. Four thick men who I have only seen scrunched up in cabs out in the fields drip a combination of sweat and flour as they rotate before the mouth of the giant woodstove I've never noticed at the back of the kitchen. The men pass between them a broad wooden pizza peel that looks like a battle axe when they bring it down on the lip of a table to shake off excess dough. I've stopped letting Baby Fox sit in my lap and Walnut has started letting him outside more often so my hands are free this evening as children squeeze in around our hips. Through some miracle of choreography and wood fire we are presented with half a pizza each. Nate and I side-eye the table as everyone folds and piles the loose dough between their teeth. It's the most food we've seen in two weeks. Before we finish, I swear that someone at the end of the table begins chanting the Falcon's name, but is quickly silenced by the big man still holding the peel.

---

5. HALL OF METALS

In the same way he foretold the Damanhurian spiritual system, Falco had visions of the Temples of Humankind at age 10. At first I didn't believe the physical structure existed, but today I regret turning down that visit. It was the community's secrecy that first inspired the Italian police to raid Damanhur, though it seems clear from Damanhur's severe contemporary bans against drug use that drugs were likely involved. The temple entrance was so well hidden that authorities threatened to dynamite the entire mountainside before Damanhurians agreed to let them en-ter. Because Damanhur had no permits for construction, the government planned to demolish the entire structure. But after images of the interior began circulating around the world on the internet, Italy and Damanhur reached a compromise.

Today Damanhur is officially self-sustaining. In 2005, the UN Global Forum on Health recognized the village as a model for sustainable society based on its architecture alone. The temples below it are said to inspire self-improvement and connection to intelligent energies of the universe.

6. HALL OF THE EARTH

"Thirty meters underground, this hall is composed of two circular rooms that create an infinity sign. This hall helps one to access the ancestral memory of our species."

On the twelfth day the Faun tells the Walnut that we will be working in a field far away. We leave before sunrise and Nate and I are the last ones out. "Quiet," the Faun urges, as I rummage through the basket where someone has so regularly forgotten to set fruit out that I've learned how to eat an apple core. I've made up with the Faun, though we are still his least favorite for reasons I do and do not understand. Hope grumbles as we climb into the truck and the Faun turns his headlights to the mountains. Up front is the Faun's girlfriend, a New Lifer whose presence is a secret here because both she and the Faun are married. Soon, half the bodies in the truck are sleeping. As we cross the first pass the Faun turns back and explains, in the way multilingual Damanhurians do to ease suspicion, that he and the Lizard are going to speak only in Italian, for now.

"Yes, there is a Time Machine in the Temple and Yes, you have to enter naked in order to travel in it. And Yes, Oberto Airaudi has had sexual relations with a large percentage of his female followers. He calls it 'alchemical magic.'"

In 2009, Oberto Airaudi was accused of tax evasion amounting to two million euros and involving "an enormous personal estate consisting of an extraordinary number of houses and bank accounts," as reported by the Çanavese newspaper *La Sentinella*. By the time we arrived in Damanhur, the community had begun to distance itself from Falco, who was developing a reputation that confirmed the Vatican's suspicions.

We stop at a convenience store wedged along the incline. We've brought no money, of course, so the Faun buys us a loaf of "American bread" wrapped in stars and stripes. It's an hour to the top and by the time the road rights itself the sun is a quarter of the way through the sky.

Maria and Hope chase sheep while the Giant takes my picture wearing Nate's hat and holding the American bread. We eat the whole thing, then the Faun and his girlfriend disappear. I lay back in the grass, noticing for the first time the way my pectoral muscles finally relax on a full stomach.

I'm wide awake by the time we get back to the dark shed and I decide to ask Nate if we can stay another week. I haven't been able to figure the place out yet. I've gotten comfortable eating alongside the little Noces and I need to ask more questions. Nate shakes his head. He's tired of the precious "energies" and can't take another day. We have eight days until our train passes expire and we're out of cash.

6. HALL OF THE EARTH 

Like many of the New Lifers we met, Fauno's girlfriend was middle aged, wealthy, and bleary eyed in the way we must have seemed during our first days in Damanhur. Most of them seemed like people struggling with a big question that they didn't want to answer. Many had left bad situations and others had lost families along the way, but all anyone talked about was how Damanhur had saved them. I've wondered since if giving yourself over to a larger power is an experience marked primarily, and at first, by relief. The New Lifers seemed ecstatic. Nate would have said they "had voices on the other line."

Damanhur Inside Out claims that Falco ordered "black magic rituals" to be carried out daily against citizens who have left the commune to discourage others from following. The authors claim that the community's land holdings have increased gradually over the years because Falco has instructed the farm Nucleo to move the fence lines gradually every night.

7. The Labyrinth 

Between 2010 and 2012, Damanhur was investigated for tax evasion and required to pay hundreds of thousands of euros in fines for medical procedures performed without license, and for psychological damage suffered by former members. In 2015, Damanhur reported that Falcon Dandelion had died due to a mysterious illness at the age of 63, though several sources speculate that the leader faked his own death.

From this distance, it has gradually become clear to me that the Emergency WWOOF job board had given us a brief loophole in an otherwise secure, decades-long pay-to-enter

At the train station we sling our backpacks up with wet boots wheeling from their straps. Walnut shakes our hands. He's got meetings in town and the goodbye is quick. "You visit next year," he tells us, eyebrows high. Then he lets his tongue hang out of the front of his mouth and exhales, I realize later, in a fox-like goodbye.

We fly out of Rome with dirt lining our nail beds and backpacks full of rank clothes. I save my last Carter story for the plane—a fairy tale about a feral woman who is raised by wolves and employed by a vampire. In a month I'll throw the small paperback away when it begins to mold. I read and I don't look out the window on our short ascent as the plane curves west, away from St. Peter's and the airspace over the Vatican, away from the Alps and the hills below them and the temples buried beneath where I know we will not return.

system. In practice this meant that we were maybe the first visitors to Damanhur who had no prior knowledge of or bias against it, yet were allowed to live and work deep inside, unchecked.

And despite everything strange, the Damanhurians had felt charming. They had each made a decision to leave something behind. Their spiritual fervor and emphasis on belonging were familiar to me, even if their language was not. The first thing to throw off any interested member is the vocabulary of a young system. Even on the surface, it seems now that a cult feels hokey because to any ear its language sounds invented, not codified. Without that surface element—the newness of the New Age—Damanhur might have really succeeded.

7. The Labyrinth 

"Walking along the Labyrinth is like walking through the entire history of humanity, distilling the divine principle from within oneself, contacting the eternal essence beyond all cultural representations."

On our last day on the farm, two weeks in, we work in the sweaty western high tunnel picking tomatoes. The crowded stalks feature net-sized spider webs. After two months in Italy's dirt and sun I still scream when I turn around carefully with a full basket and brush my shoulder against a black and yellow spider the size of a ripe tomato, expectant at the center of her web. The Faun looks disappointed. Soon Walnut is calling me from the front of the house and I have to extricate myself from the whole situation and climb out of the tunnel carefully. The Faun translates because the Walnut is frantic. "He says Baby Fox has been missing for two days. He wants to know if you have seen him." "No," I admit, as the Fairy gives me an unwelcome squeeze from behind.

INTO THE LIMEN: WHERE AN

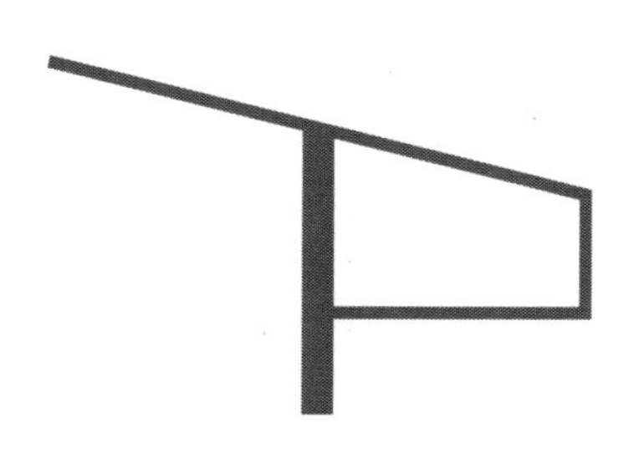

OLD SQUIRREL GOES TO DIE

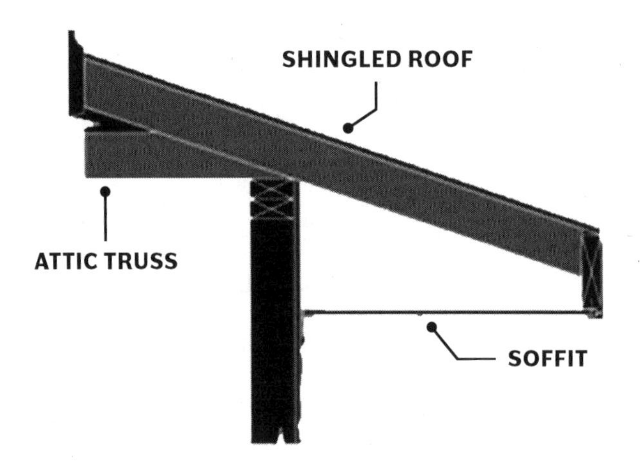
SHINGLED ROOF
ATTIC TRUSS
SOFFIT

I.

A **soffit** is an architectural element resulting from the combination of two dissimilar spaces. It is the under or inside of a construction component such as an arch, a flight of stairs, a ceiling space, or the exposed surface beneath a section of roof that bridges the gap between a house's siding and roofline, otherwise known as the eaves.

A.

2. For the past 50 years, my family has lived in what's known as the Lambert-Musser house on West Second Street in Muscatine. It's a three-story late Victorian that sits among others on a bluff above the Mississippi, just across from Illinois. The walls are grey frame weatherboard and the

1.

The man calls
himself "The Critter Gitter."
He has seven fingers and "not many teeth,"
says my grandmother, offhand, worrying the high collar
of her fleece. When I meet Jim on the back steps he greets me without a
handshake, keeping knuckles at rest along the hip of his jeans. He has the kind of dry tan
that doesn't fade. The hollows of his cheeks are suede-like and wrinkled as palms. He has the rope-thin look of a sailor and wears the tattoo of a black pheasant in flight along his forearm, a Bass belt buckle, a lisp.

In my first few minutes with Jim I resume the bad habit I've had all my life, the one of asking hasty, precise questions about a stranger's profession, which reads as if I'm starved for work and on the immediate market for anything, though this has only now and then been the case. I ask Jim what it looks like inside ceilings, how he gets in there, what a squirrel's tail feels like, if I can take notes. My grandmother addresses me with an insistent, knowing look but Jim begins to speak quickly, treating me as a kind of job-shadower, and maybe I sort of am one, so I don't elaborate.

Snappy old-timers call Muscatine, Iowa, "both the west coast and the east bank" of the Mississippi. I'm visiting my grandparents there to research the town's pearl button industry. When I wake the first morning in my mother's old bedroom there is a quality to the paneled sunlight that tells of snow. But it's June, I remember, and soon a scuttling picks up in the ceiling, and then the event that woke me—black dust spurting from the air vent, clouding the foot of my quilt. "Attic squirrels," says my grandmother from the hall. They cut a tree down last month, but still, she's calling someone, so I carry a ladder from the carriage house up the soggy, carpeted steps as my lithe granny jogs behind. I pluck my fingers from the slats that tick and pinch and crank the vent tight as we wait for Jim to arrive.

roof is shingled asphalt. It has a skinny side yard and a red brick chimney and a second-story glass porch where my grandparents sleep uninsulated and facing the river in all seasons. Daniel Lambert, attorney, built the trunk of the house in 1866, three decades before the button boom came to give the Pearl City its nickname. When the Lamberts fell on hard times they sold the place at a Sheriff's auction, and the house lay vacant, furnished but uninhabited, for almost a decade. Then the lumber baron, Clifton R. Musser, bought the place in 1904, the year the caterpillar tread was invented to allow the tank and the verdant steel thresher to roll continuously. Musser was head of the Weyerhaeuser Timber Company and President of the Muscatine Bank. He built the brick stable and auto house at the back of the property. He added a solarium, a small elevator, and an attic to what Lambert had made. He planted five pines in the backyard, of the same species his company stripped from the banks not a mile away before floating them down the river.

3. For 10 years an area of six square feet slept inside the wall at the crown of my head and I never knew its color. Then, on a morning in April, my father left our house and his life there and the next spring the rest of us followed suit, with the dog, in a truck. We left our dents on the corners, a box on the high shelf, our layer of paint like a new tree ring. There are bits of my skin that stayed there. Long hairs still wound into carpet, our echoes caught up in the walls.

When a house is measured in square feet, there are places unaccounted for. Cabinets and bathtubs open into recesses where no wall leans its back against another. Some areas get sealed just after being built and not aired again until disaster or demolition. A house is like a coat with holes in its pockets. I wonder about its intangible additions, about the wild and functional places behind walls that listen to and collect us. These margins that belong to less human things.

B.

5. In 1959 when Musser's widow, Margaret, was moved to a retirement facility, the windows on Second Street darkened for another decade. In those years my grandmother Sarah had two babies that she bathed in a double-bowl sink on 8th Street, lower on the bluff where houses were cheap. The

4. Jim carries a flashlight, a catch pole, and a pair of gauntlet gloves. When we step onto the back porch he sits slowly and leans elbows to knees. He's a talker and a smoker and the conversation between us is oddly familiar because of his steady ease, but I lurch around what I want to ask him. This house is where my sister and I were sent when we needed to disappear during our parents' divorce. Like the time when our mom was hospitalized for dehydration or when our parents left the country separately. But I get the feeling that Jim knows the place better than we do. I want to ask him about the short doors at the backs of closets, those manholes to the house. I want him to hand over maps of all the inner territories. But my questions feel crazed and intimate when I realize that it could matter to me if those depths were finite and barren. Instead I ask Jim about common pests as he takes a short drag and sucks air to top it off.

J: Well, they get into crawlspaces, vents in the attic. Raccoons look for dark spots along a roof and climb up. A racoon'll hunch herself up under a soffit and stand up on her hind legs to push the metal away. Then she'll rip out the wires and insulation.
S: Soffit? Is that a kind of room?
J: (Pointing) See? Where the roof attaches to the house, that triangular space. That's not part of any room. It's a very intimidating place for a person. Dead airspace with a pitch to the roof.
S: In our old house there was this tiny door in the attic leading to this hallway lined with sheet metal. There was a turn at the end but I never went far enough to see past.
J: Oh well that's where you'll find the raccoon. It's mostly like that. Metal and wires. Sometimes it gets hard to breathe. This real fine, heavy dust, almost silver. You can see tracks real clear. There's lotsa cobwebs, mice. We're so big compared to a critter ya know? But it's the perfect place for them, safe and warm. It gets about 120 degrees, so you don't wanna pass out, and the only way out is the way you come in, so you don't wanna get turned around neither. Wasps too, they'd kill you right there in the attic if you got stuck.
S: Do you ever feel scared?
J: 'Course, sometimes. Sometimes there's just short planks that lay across ceiling joints to walk on. When a raccoon comes charging out of the dark you have two choices, to fight or flee. Once I fell clean through the ceiling. The critter run me outta there! That's why I got insurance. But I never been bitten, and I've got a couple thousand of 'em . . . No, that's not true! I got bit by a dang ground squirrel once, blood and everything.

I grimace and try to hide it but Jim snickers.

first baby, my mother Margaret, was named after her grandmother like I am. My grandfather calls her "The Peach," his wife "Cherry," and me "#2." He and my grandmother weren't looking to move, but something about the old house made them pick up and invest. They bought it for 35k with a loan from my great grandfather, but when they arrived they found the house in a state of partial decay. The place had been unkempt for many years before it was abandoned, and the Mussers had taken nothing but personal effects. Moth-eaten drop cloths described heavy sofas and cabinets. The closets were stacked with linens yellowing along the fold. My grandparents didn't have much so they kept most of what could be salvaged. Growing up, I sat in Musser armchairs, read by their lamplight, sounded the creaks they wore into floors. They linger in shelves of books that disintegrate when pulled from the shelf, in lacquered toys in the corner of the basement, in chairs with hand-carved feet. Sometimes my grandmother brings out pieces of Musser crystal at holidays and the family may as well be upright at the table with us.

6.

If a lineage
is measured by a lingering
aesthetic in china settings and eyes that
reflect a river, then the Mussers are some version of our
ancestors. Their possessions are hallowed, their stories significant to
ours. We speak about them haltingly, but keep their trunks of photographs in the attic in case someone comes back after all this time. As a kid I knew that reverence, as if parts of the house was never ours, as if somewhere there were rooms kept back. My family was contracting and I had a lot of time. I felt for buried hallways where the doorframes didn't match. I pressed my eye to cracks that might filter light into rooms where our voices had blended with pocket change and socks, floss and silver. Today when I look into a split wall I still think of that state as wreckage, as if all deep interiors should be furnished for the purpose of collecting.

C.

8. The house that my parents left separately stood on a hill in Illinois. It was another first investment. Double-porched and river-facing and in rough shape, the house had five entrances left over from the years it spent divided into apartments. On two sides were graveyards and on the third, a highway. The tall attic had a bricked-over fireplace with a

7. Jim is trying hard not to curse around me, but he's also trying to get me to laugh. I gather that he could talk for hours, and that among his talents Jim is a seasoned salesman and a storyteller, roles that may prove interdependent in a town where every conversation has a cellar.

S: Do you ever find anything in those extra places? Like furniture?
J: Never furniture. Those aren't really spots where people went to, you know, socialize. Once I crawled way back in an attic and found a big trunk. I asked the guy if he wanted me to bring it down. He had to be about 75. It was a box of his grandfather's pictures from college in the 1920s that he'd never seen. All yellow. He was surprised. Folks don't even know what's inside their own habitat. I find tools a lot too. A chisel or a file, jack planes and hammers, things that workers left behind.
S: Do you carry those out too?
J: No ho. I always put the tools back, I tell 'em right where it is, but I leave it just there. Sometimes dead animals too. I found a perfect squirrel skeleton in your grandma's attic once. Completely intact.
S: Really? Here? Was it rotting?
J: No just like that. Bare bones, nothing left. You can't tell at the time, all that smell gets vented out the roof.
S: Do you think something ate it?
J: No, no, multiple generations living in there. That's why I keep comin' back here every time. They think this is their home now. Where does an old squirrel go to die? He goes where he lives.

strange ringing around it, as if the space remembered being lit. It was lined with low, wide windowsills that smelled of beetle shells and sunbaked dust. The stairs creaked and the heating popped and sung. As soon as the wind was kept out it found a new way in. Our father worked late and left early and my mother and I kept our eyes ahead as we locked up each one of the big doors at night. We didn't talk God, or death, or the reasons for a haunt. Even in Illinois, we were Iowans. We didn't have to look directly at anything to know it was there. This was the year Mom picked up our hands and walked out of church during a sermon the pastor was delivering to make her and my father an example. She dropped twenty pounds and bought a leopard print dress. This was the year I told her that one day I would buy our house from whomever was living there and put everything back the way it was and she told me that I might need to speak with a psychiatrist about that someday. We moved back to Iowa, forty minutes from Muscatine, where my grandparents held Christmas parties and invited everyone in town. My friends and I worked coat check in party dresses and snuck tumblers of Sprite and champagne into the elevator shaft. We pulled the rusty door shut, jammed the emergency stop, and got first-drunk in the space between floors. Within a year my sister and I had a new father, two new brothers, and a new-new house stale with plaster.

9.

Bachelard writes:
"Thus we cover the universe with drawings we have lived. These drawings need not be exact. They need only to be tonalized in the mode of our inner space." Always, I dream inside houses where I have lived or loved someone. Most often, the interiors splice my grandparents' and parents' first homes haphazardly. The floors of the two houses alternate, their first story, our second. For a year, bits of my boyfriend's family home attached itself to my old one. Staircases and their landings extend into others, triple jointed. Additions of other houses bloom from hallways like extra limbs. To my sleeping brain all seems navigable, familiar. My mother and sister don't dream this way, though they both admit that they never want to live in the first iteration of a home.

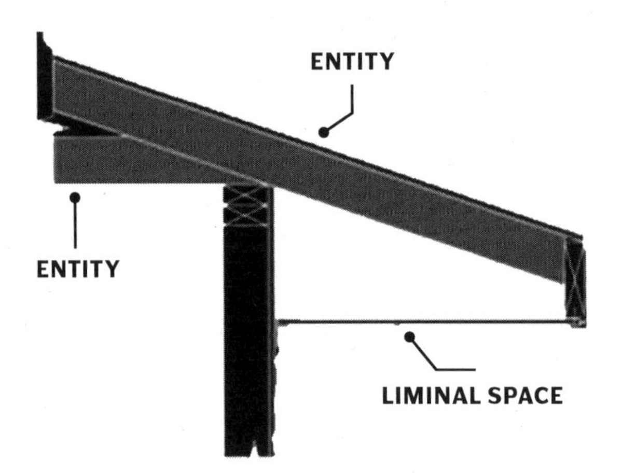
ENTITY
ENTITY
LIMINAL SPACE

II.

A **liminal space** is an ambiguous zone between two definitive entities as applied to both spatial and temporal dimensions. It is a space or state that simultaneously divides and unites and exists only in the presence of an outer and inner, a perceived set of doubles. When two planes meet, it's the limen that remains between. Or, when a cabinet door fits loose in its socket, the liminal space is the ever-present gap, however miniscule, that persists. Airports are liminal spaces, as are shorelines, porches, puberties, graveyards, drag shows, skins, comas, and stepsiblings.

D.

11. Sometimes the hunting dogs are smiling and cataracted and greying at their tips and sometimes they are massive, sloppy pups that shake the door hinges as I approach the old house. There are always exactly two of them, and my grandmother always

10.

S: So how do you catch them—what do you do with the animals afterwards?
J: You know, you have to think like a raccoon sometimes. I have to be patient. Some folks think I can just blow a flute and the critter will come running to the cage. You know, I have to go in with what I call "extreme prejudice," because sometimes the folks just want the critter eliminated.

Jim looks at me without blinking, couching his answer in a way I will come to think of as his mode of gauging a listener's politics.

S: So . . . sometimes you kill them.

Jim looks at me gravely, and then at his hands.

J: Yes. I don't have malice, I love animals. Sometimes I get real emotional.
S: Yeah, I'm into animals too.
J: You gotta have emotions. It's a real necessary thing! The job's not for everyone. You've gotta have some mustard. You have to be outgoing. It's a kinda entrepreneurial thing.
S: Brave?
J: Yes, brave. My grandpa used to say "grow a hair!" that meant buck up and get in there, get that thing! You have to look at your fears. Get the critter where it waits.
S: Well, it sounds like you've had time to practice.
J: I mean, I have a lot of experience. But I still have to, you know, mentally prepare, come in with my extreme prejudice, as I say. I pray that it's not a damnable practice. Once I had to take out 11 adult raccoons. That was a terrible thing. I've cried when I had to eliminate a family with baby foxes, too. There's a fox downtown that I know, I know right where his hole is in the middle of town, but no one else knows and I'm not gonna say nothing.

needs to walk them to the park. Then we cook or pick out frames together or troubleshoot at the desktop. She always has an afternoon meeting with folks who call themselves "grassroots volunteers" before we dress for dinner and go get stewed at some empty restaurant, having a loud conversation that I always try to hush. So it's no surprise when we end up alone in the Thai place that night, at the hour my family calls "wine o'clock." They kick us out long after close and back at the top of the hill we are breathless and tipsy and she wants to walk out to the cliff and look over the river. This part is new. A tugboat chases its spotlight against the current, pushing hard at five barges and one long horn. In the months between the duplex and Second Street, my mother's family lived in an old clammer house on stilts that the Mussers rented out as they got their affairs in order. The Peach says the sound of this barge horn is the first thing she remembers.

12. A place
that can't be measured gets
erased by its descriptions. Which is why I can't
separate the idea of ghosts from these spaces. These spots
nested just beyond the path of the inhabitant. I know that houses keep our
bits, but they also get stuck with our decisions. Some do regret. This is what makes a ghost—the remnants of several lives and a place for them to gather quietly. This is the way a house knows. Why it aches at the stairwell. This is what's meant by something lingering at the threshold like a soul.

14. I go for a tired run along the Muscatine Riverwalk lit by cloudy vintage bulbs. The wind from the river brings the reek of moldering fish and the briny, electric scent of an incoming storm. I take a hot shower and search my mother's drawers for lip balm. The white built-ins have rows of

13.

S: Do you ever think you'll see a ghost?

This is the first time Jim doesn't answer me straight away. Instead he sits back in his chair, folds his cigarette across his belt buckle, and holds my gaze.

J: I look for them. It's strange, my brain knows I'm back in a place where no one has been maybe in a century. I wonder who was here, and ya know they're gone now, but they were the last ones before you.
S: Right.

Jim motions to the neighborhood.

J: Some of these old mansions, you just don't know. I've been startled a few times. I hear a sound real close and turn around, and nothing's there! But a ghost won't make a noise, that's what I tells myself.
S: Is that why you don't take the tools?
J: Yep. These planks have gone to shit, but those are somebody's!

He takes a sip of water from the bottle at his hip as I write quickly. I begin a question and my grandma steps through the glass door to tell me we better get going. We're late for our dinner down the hill. I stand up and Jim smiles and there's a pause and a lurch. A near-hug that we turn from, sheepish.

J: You know, you could come up there with me, if Grandma's okay with it.

A bit of static between my shoulders takes me by surprise—I'm scared. The eyes of the house are trying to catch mine. My grandma raises her eyebrows slowly while I falter. "Another time?" she says, thinking I need an out. "Another time?" I look at Jim and he nods. We clasp left hands and hold for a second. "Nice to talk with you." "You too."

Jim hands me a card. He lifts his tools toward the craggy back staircase and looks over his shoulder. "You give me a ring!" he says, winking.

keyholes that stretch to the ceiling. I climb on the sink to reach the highest, snooping, and find small wicker baskets of brittle hairpins, pill boxes, silk jewelry bags, dried-out perfume that could be from '56 though the smudged 5 is maybe a 7. It's been 30 years since my mom and her brother moved out and left my grandparents to themselves. Thirty years with just the two of them and three floors of centenarian house. Lately, my grandparents drive the 40 minutes to us for holidays. They garden and sit by the fire, they get another puppy they can't train. They've been losing control of the place for some time and none of us knows what's packed into the varied storage. We're wondering quietly how long it will be until we need to open the hatches. It seems like my grandma might go the way Margaret did, watching each room slip beneath dust until she is the last thing to leave. Most people no longer die in their houses. Our name will not be added to the Lambert-Musser chain. We built no tangible additions. We shored things up. We sifted into the fissures they made long before.

15. In many old houses a slit was made in the back of medicine cabinets for disposing used razor blades. This is why remodelers sometimes encounter a cascade of antique blades. Some turn of the century homes also came with "wall hives" which kept bees and their honey close at hand, and sometimes persist long after they have been sealed inside a house. More than sharp edges, stingers and teeth, close darkness, what I'm afraid of about these crawlspaces are the things they might know. I worry that something lies forgotten there that doesn't want to be left alone. This feels like the guilt I have knowing I won't be the one to take up the house for the very reason that houses like this usually go to ruin. For their size and their dying towns and the cost of their upkeep. I worry about a future time when the old place gets divided or knocked down, when our remnants have nowhere to go.

F.

16.

When I finally call,
Jim's reluctant to make plans. The
only weekend I'm available is the first of deer
season. He tells me I should go on up my own.

J: It ain't that scary. Some people asked me once if I was afraid of ghosts goin' into old houses. They musta been watching those paranormal shows or something.
S: Jim, that was me who asked you. When we first met!
J: Oh ho! Well sometimes I think about it now. You know when I go into a place, now I talk to the house sometimes.
S: Yeah?
J: I says, I'm here to help. Those critters are gonna chew you to hell inside. I'm like a doctor coming in to stop the bad stuff.

Two weeks later, Jim meets me on the porch with a pointed skull in hand. My grandma is at her Grassroots meeting, and the house is ours to crawl through unsupervised.

J: Look what I brought ya, I thought you might like it.
S: What is it?
J: It's a badger, them's about the meanest animals we got in this state. See these canines?
S: Yikes. Did you find it somewhere?
J: No, I caught this one by the golf course bothering some people.
S: On a golf course? So you skinned it?
J: No, I just boiled it clean to get the skull, like a cat. You know the best way to catch a coyote is to get a cat. They can't resist a cat.
S: Do you let the cats . . . go? After they serve as bait?
J: Well. You know . . . You don't use a live cat for trapping. Easier to get one dead.

Jim tells me about things he traps accidentally. About how, at the humane society he is known as "the bounty hunter." This gentle trapper is letting me see a different side. This time, I've brought a digital recorder and a bit more gumption. Jim is curious too, but he's performing more this time. He has good lines and he knows it. *Git* is a part of the language he uses for effect to peddle the Critter Gitter like an alias to the people who want someone to crawl behind their walls and come back out.

17. After my mother's family settled in at Second Street, the Mussers' daughter, Margaret II, asked to come back and visit three times. My mother's room had been hers, and though she hadn't lived there for years, my grandma said she had loved the house so much she needed to see it every so often. Later, Margaret Musser died in a car accident and only afterwards did my grandparents find a stack of her letters in the back of one of the cabinets.

18.

Margaret is the name of
my mother, her grandmother, and me
by middle name. Three more have come and gone
among the Mussers. Most of us have lived in the white bedroom on
the second floor. I look into the dimpled mirror, the one as old as the house, and
imagine all our faces in there, as if the house could know the difference.

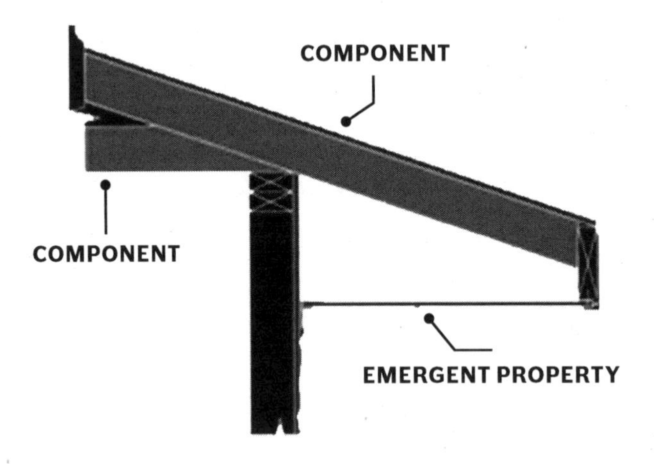
COMPONENT
COMPONENT
EMERGENT PROPERTY

III.

An **emergent property** is one that results when simple components are joined in constraining relations to produce a unique element that is present in neither of the individual elements. This concept is captured by the phrase, "the whole is greater than the sum of its parts." Consciousness is an emergent property resulting from the combined parts of the human brain; we do not know where or how it resides, only that it does when these parts combine. Examples from nature include hive mentality, and the pulsing of hundreds of fireflies in tandem. To highlight emergence at work, we might look to a soffit, the internet, collaborations, or a nest built between eaves.

19.

We start in the
basement. The recorder in
my front pocket digs into a hip crease
while the industrial beam swings from Jim's hand,
showing me exactly what he's looking at. We crawl upwards
through the house. I choose the route and Jim narrates, his rough voice
itinerant through the recording. We find pipes cushioned in asbestos, a silver shaving
mirror receding into black, a special hand drill for punching button rounds from clamshells, a toilet unhitched from its plumbing. I lift a hatch while Jim sticks his head down the laundry chute and yells his report, "Hoses, powerlines, debris, don't guillotine me please!" Then Jim shows me where he caught the first squirrels in the attic.

J: I trapped 'em here with the wedding dresses. They ate a hole through the ceiling up there, and they were climbin' all over the clothes and makin' a mess. I set some cages and it took a while, but I did get 'em and your grandma was real happy.

We crawl inside our first soffit on the third floor, through a door about a third of Jim's height.

J: This is one of those, what did you say, indigenous spaces?
S: Yeah. Liminal, actually.
J: Well, the critter, he'd be right around that corner, maybe you're gonna find something there.
S: Back there?
J: Yep. You gotta watch and not step in a hole, if you step through that one there you'll go right through the ceiling.

I inch down the triangular, exposed hall, empty but for scattered acorns and what looks very much like a fleshy down comforter stuffed between the beams.

J: This pink stuff, you know, this is fiberglass. It itches, and you don't necessarily really want to stir it up too bad . . .
S: Fiberglass, got it. Is that a kind of insulation?
J: Well lookit, they really chewed the hell out of . . . No, fiberglass is really a new stuff. This grey matter insulation you see here, that's shredded-up newspaper, cellulose fiber stuffed in a lining. Old stuff, extras.
S: Grey matter, hm.

20. Certain traits skip generations, bloodlines, helix railings. My mother swears emphatically that she has never seen a ghost. "Yuck," she says, when I ask. "Let's not talk about creepy things." On the way back to the house, my grandmother wants to be straight, "You know, I can't really say. A ghost doesn't sound like a nice thing. Isn't that about revenge? I'm not sure about seeing anything but I hear sounds over the years. It's just me here a lot. Makes you wonder what's been going on. They're not bad things. Mostly I say it's just the dogs." Maybe it's the spirits, the conversation, the cold night, but when we sway back up the hill and into our beds I'm not as wary of sleeping in my mother's room, of my inherited vacancies and what they contain.

21.

"The state of your house is the state of your mind," my mother would nag when I insisted that my room was cozier beneath a layer of paper leaves and clothing. Her aphorism seemed intended to induce the organization of both spaces, but mostly it just made me feel shameful about revealing my most inner struggles so obviously in the arrangement of my things.

H.

23. The storm ends and clouds disperse like rubble in the sky. It's time to leave the grey house again. Time to drive the 40 minutes back to my city and the life advancing there. Before I go, my

22.
Up in the attic
we peel apart cartoon-sized
cobwebs, our voices on the recording edging
into focus as the house begins to taper and constrain.

J: Yeah the squirrels were drivin' her nuts here and she thought, well this guy's an interesting character.
S: Well . . . you do have an interesting job.
J: Yes I'm sure that's exactly what she thought. Yeah that! (pointing at a ladder leading into a door in the ceiling) The skeleton is up there.
S: It is? Now?
J: Well, no . . . I took it a course. Watch your eyes, cause there's dirt. (scuffling) So let's see. Well, that hinges back real easy, and it's not gonna hurt you, so you can just push it open with your head. And just go easy and then you can shine the light in there. And you can see why . . . why I didn't wanna crawl in.
S: (climbing) Okay . . .
J: (snickers) When they call you and say ooh yeah Jim I want you to catch that squirrel for me, and you have to go into a space like that . . .
S: Um, can I have the light? I'm not tall enough to . . .
J: Just take another step and put your back against that door. The skeleton was in that hole there.
S: (scuffling) Ugh. And what's all the stuff hanging down?
J: Well, let me see, can I sneak up on the ladder?

Jim and I perch together on a single rung with our heads between the ceiling and the roof. It smells of rot and the heat is oppressive even in October. I direct my beam onto the materials that hang about our ears. Tar paper. A patch of dead moss. Electrical wires threaded through glass insulators and abandoned. A lead water tank riveted to the rafters.

J: The thing is when they redone the heating and stuff, they couldn't get this son of a gun out.
S: And what's this? (pointing up) Is it like a handle? For holding on?
J: Yep I guess so . . . No . . . That looks like a hatch.
S: What?
J: It's a hatch! To the roof!
S: Okay . . . wait? Can we . . . ?
J: You can get that out of . . .
S: Can we just push it . . . ?
J: Grandma ain't gonna get mad . . . ?
S: No no no she said we can go . . .
J: Careful, cuz you don't wanna . . .
(wind) (light)

grandma wrenches an orange binding from deep in bookshelves. It's a book by Margaret's daughter, Marion Musser. A handwritten note inside the cover reads: "Dear Rodger and Sarah, Since this tale starts in your house, I thought you might be interested. It comes with all good wishes for you and yours for the new millennium. Cordially, Marion. Jan. 2000." "I was born in our house at West Second Street," Marion begins, "In Muscatine, Iowa on September 11, 1910—at least my Uncle George testified to that when I applied for my first passport, as there were no birth certificates then." Marion describes her father who called her "peaches," and tells the story of a Muscatine boy who once told her that he'd overheard men plotting to kidnap her and hide her on a boat going down the Mississippi for ransom. She writes about her travels to more than twenty countries as a woman in the early '40s.

24. Soffits, it turns out, are pretty treacherous. They feel like somewhere between an animal den and a back alley. During construction builders often use them for trash, which is easier to wall in than remove. Soffits guard nests and banned poisons, oiled newspapers, jagged metal scraps. A soffit measures time indoors the way a landfill can. It chronicles eras of retired technology, dust that rises like flood lines along a bank. Even the air decays. Inside these spaces it is plain that, before they described a house, the walls were once soil, and they are on their way back to becoming soil again. Lately, in describing third-spaces, I've been thinking in colors. Black seemed easy, the color of being sealed, the absence of light, but I've decided on grey, which contains nearly the entire spectrum, but reads as empty. Brain matter. It houses all the hues we can and will never perceive.

25.

S: Okay, comin' up.

J: There.

(a train whistle)

S: You can see the river bend from here.

J: Grandma prolly never done that!

S: No, I don't know if anyone's done this in a while.

(wind)

S: Is it okay to walk on this roof?

J: Just don't get near the edge. Cause you can, what can happen is, is a . . . there's a funny phenomenon, you just go to the edge you'll automatically want to go over it. It's really weird, I can't explain it.

S: Yeah I . . . sometimes I write about that feeling.

J: Ah there's a chimney cap up here, or the raccoons would be right in there!

S: Ah, yeah.

J: And turds.

S: Really.

J: Yeah, he'd be like, hey this is my new territory, and then he'd crap all over.

Jim sits and lights a cigarette and I ask him if I can have one.

J: Well, are you gonna get in trouble?

S: No.

J: How old are you?

S: Twenty-five.

J: Yeah, you most certainly can have one. (holding up lighter) You just put that on there. Watch it.

Jim tells me about thinking like an animal; always having an escape route. About dogs he's seen jump straight off a cliff. He talks about finding his grandfather's newspapers boxed up in a family barn. About his life in Iowa and his soft spot for forgotten things. On the roof, with smoke between us, I consider that I'm following a man who traps animals for a living through my family's historic home. Officially, Jim is an exterminator for whom the animal is alternately a pest, a product, and an intimate body deserving of respect. He knows how to divide a carcass and boil its bones, and he'd probably rather be doing that right now. Jim owns black dogs, roots for my teams, and traces his roots to this river city. But I'm an amateur researcher enrolled in an arts program, and he's an expert in the backwoods and the wild indoors. Jim grew up trapping his food three decades before I was raised in a suburban neighborhood. And now he's here, doing his job, sitting beside me on a roof built by lumber barons, telling me about friends of his that live under the bridges downtown. Friends, he says, who'd be happy to move into the carriage house, as we dangle our legs over the gutters and watch the black dogs scuff holes in the yard. We look down into the house and close the hatch up behind us. This time when he leaves, Jim doesn't wink. We shake right hands for the first time, my fingers gripping haphazardly around his knuckles and into empty space.

26. The time is wine o'clock and I'm home at the bar with my mother, describing the innards of her childhood house. She seems lacking interest, or perhaps disappointed, as I admit that I am too. It's not that the crawlspaces of my mind and those we clambered into are mutually exclusive, exactly. I came out carrying old medicine bottles without threads, stacks of photos from both my family and the Mussers', a silk glove, three shotgun shells, bites on my ankles and wrists from some infesting insect, coatings of dust that alternated by century, and some sounds—a human-like hum on the recording that we didn't hear while shuffling around. But I didn't see squirrels, and no ghosts followed me home. In stepping beyond hatches meant to be sealed forever, what we found, mostly, were a lot of unsightly things.

27.
A soffit is home undomesticated. A place for strangers to mend. A place for unlikely encounters, where boundaries get thin. Comfortable at the animal level, collecting at the human. And maybe what we heard there were squirrels in the walls—the dust was from their bones after all, and never ours. But a house collects more than tangible artifacts and grows with its inhabitants—a process somewhere between the way a snail shell adds spiraling rims as an inner mollusk expands, and the way shells of various crabs are discarded, and gather new tenants. Of this I am assured. I was a small thing myself, once added into these rooms.

A LOG CABIN SQUARE

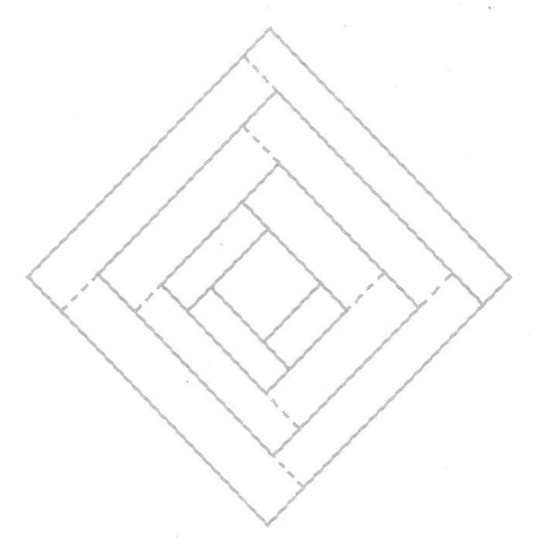

"A Log Cabin Square" can also be read at: **HTTPS://THEDIAGRAM.COM/18_2/MINOR.HTML**

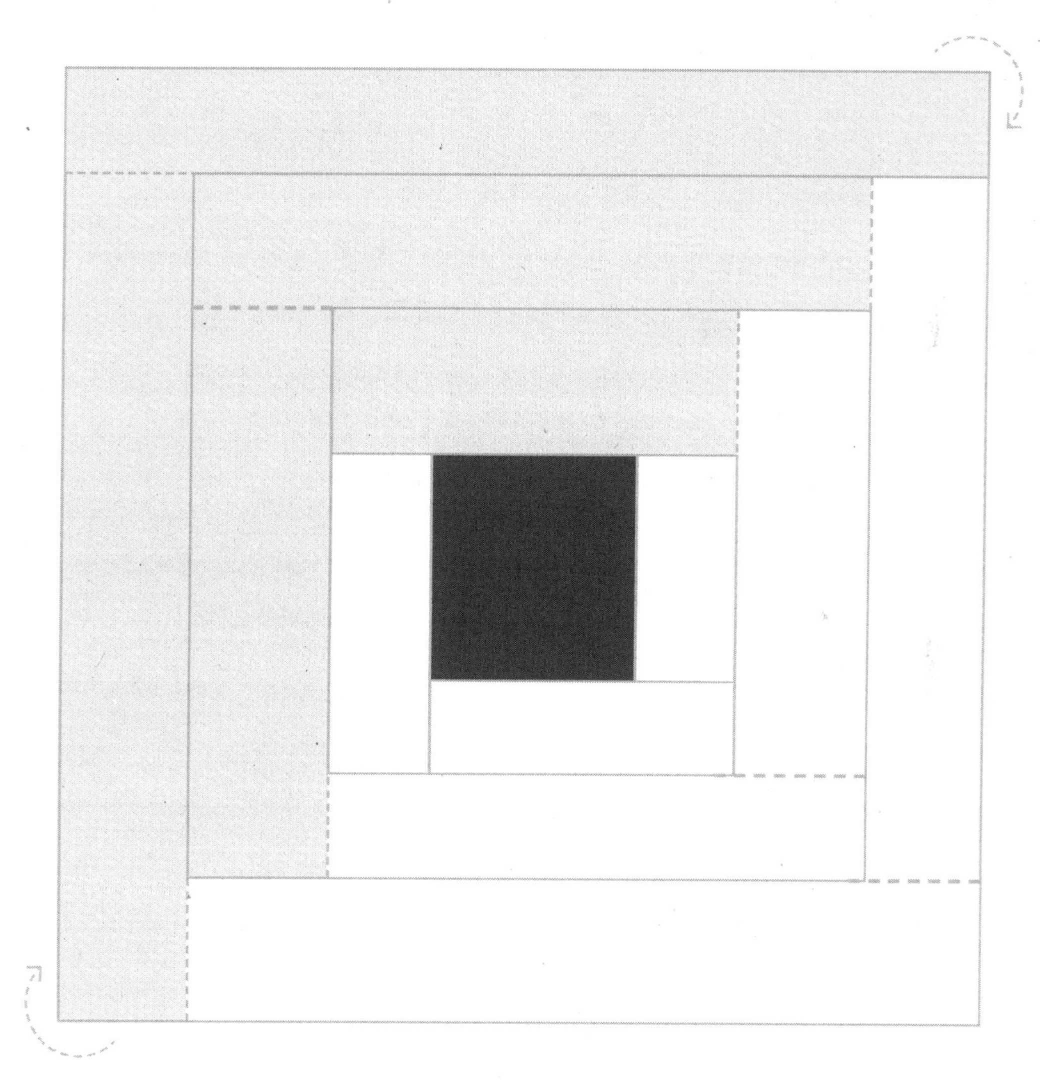

“A Log Cabin Square” can also be read at: **HTTPS://THEDIAGRAM.COM/18_2/MINOR.HTML**

MISSISSIPPI PEARL:

I.

"A pearl is a calcareous body composed of concentric layers around a central nucleus, and organically produced by a living mollusk, a soft-bodied invertebrate animal bearing a hard, external (**SHELL**)."

A natural pearl never starts as a single grain of sand, but it can begin when a mollusk is invaded by a minute foreign body—like a pebble, a weft of algae, or a doomed larvae—and responds by coating the invader with iridescent, shell-forming tissue known as nacre, or mother of pearl, to cushion its tender flesh. That new pearl becomes an extension of the mollusk's exoskeleton—its clunky shell. A pearl is a spit wad wound to temper a blister; an analog of defense mechanisms.

Pearls grow in organ-like places. We could argue that human kidney stones are also a type of pearl. The ones we wear are created by mollusks, the second most diverse animal group on earth after insects with more than 100,000 living species. Shellfish are the best pearl makers simply because they contain more surface area along their fleshy, ruffled bodies than an animal like the land snail, whose organs are tightly coiled into spiraling halls where light rarely extends itself. The crevices inside a looser shellfish capture potential pearls that catch between organs during the animal's near constant filtering of water for food. Pearls aren't deadly to a shellfish, but (**PRYING**) open a mollusk to remove its pearl will surely kill the animal by severing structures that built the coveted object for self-protection.

(**SHELL**: The last
time I died, I bled out. I used
to imagine they were blow darts, a few in
the ribs, some old black poison scoring every dorsal
vein. Or else plague rats nibbled at my sores, taking turns
and pressing noses as I breathed in some medieval alley. Stay with
me and let's say the old wives were right. If you listen to Dr. Ian Stevenson, Harvard Division of Perceptual Studies, my last life ended when I was
punctured 13 times in my right side, in the place where I now wear a set of 13
large moles. Exsanguination, it's called, bleeding out. Maybe I was the nestling
tipped into mulberries past my mother's window. Or my own Grandad's iron sights
constellated holes in my brown flank. Before it got a bad name, storytelling was
one way to explain the unfathomable. Narratives were among our few tools against
death, and sometimes they did save us. In 1930, an oral story that had been passed
across 10 generations advised Papua New Guineans to climb to the highest point
of land when sea levels dropped low and certain species swam far into open
water. Some heads of families groaned, but everyone climbed together,
saving all but 0.1% of the population after the catastrophic tsunami
that followed. It's oral stories that say a birthmark or mole tells of
the way a child last died. In traditions like those, the ones I
was raised in, a story is like an entry in the almanac.
A defense that passes the way blood does,
condensing along the way.)

(**PRYING**:
Above my desk is mounted the
cross-section of a clamshell, something I ripped
from a science periodical in a drawing studio the same year
I cared abysmally for an aquatic snail in a low-oxygen bowl in my
dorm room. I later discovered my snail was carnivorous when it sucked
a smaller other-species of snail from the tiny barren shell it left on the
cobalt pebbles under a faux roman archway, like an offering. In that
paper remnant, black and white cross-hatched organs are
stuck with lines like pins labeling the anatomy in
both English and Chinese.)

(**LINEAGE**:
Birthmarks, as the name suggests, are moles that show up before or just after birth. Mine is a moley family. Our moles have to do with our habits regarding daylight and with the waltz between helixes before the sun hits us. Our moles persist across generations. We earn them and we pass them. My sister was born moleyest of all, and had tiny spots that darkened even her earlobes and nostril, mistaken for rings until she pierced both places. Later she had two oblong sun-moles cut out from beneath her collarbones when a pinch-nosed dermatologist worried they were cancerous. The surgeons who botched the procedure left her with a pair of delicate, cross-hatched scars in the shape of fossils where the stitches had lain and I coveted those marks. They were new skin made in the shape of something ancient.)

(**SHARD**:
Slugs, leeches, conchs and squid are mollusks. They each work like a muscular kidney and their brains encircle their esophagus. A full revolution within them is called a whorl. Maybe a deep affinity for mollusks marks a curiosity for imnards, wrong- sides-out, for dark meat, for secrets held in the gut.)

(**LIGHT**: From the way he walks you can tell my father is a man who wanted sons. These days he often lies flat as physicians dig out bits of dermal tissue that saw dozens of summers in Carolina without SPF. Because I share his complexion, I wasn't allowed to apply my own sunscreen until I turned 18. Instead I'd wait in the shady house until everyone left for the beach and my father found the SPF 30. His palm would be gritty from morning sand as he held my wrist away with one hand and spread lotion firmly with the other. My suit straps undone, my legs unshaved. Then, at 45, my father had a growth removed from above his left eyebrow. The suture pulled his skin tight and left him with one brow arched, quizzical, and my sister and I laughed until the skin re-stretched. As an adult I slather myself in the small, cornered, swimsuit places, and I wear a wide brim outdoors, but my moles still dilate. My skin puckers where the light got to me.)

Linnaeus earned the "von" in his noble title not for his work with nomenclature, but for pioneering and mastering a technique for culturing round pearls. The only difference between a cultured pearl and the natural kind is planned (**LINEAGE**). In pearl culturing, an object is selected and gently introduced into the living mollusk that grows in a controlled environment until it bears the desired shape. In Linnaeus's methods, as in today's large-scale pearl cultures, the introduced object is often a (**SHARD**) of an older, discarded mollusk's shell.

Like all prosperous trades, the history of pearls is bloody. Because pearl-making mollusks have luminescent shells, they were first exchanged whole, as currency, in native societies. During the 20th century button boom those same shellfish were harvested by the tens of thousands to be scraped clean and punched of iridescent disks that were polished and slipped through soft buttonholes across the world.

But nacre, by design, is never meant to encounter the sun—least of all in view of predators. Consider that pearlescence is a mirage, a trick produced when the human eye looks through hundreds of translucent layers many times thinner than tissue—a thickness close to the wavelength of light—and instead of the three-dimensional cross-section licked by a shellfish over its lifetime, we perceive a shifting spectrum. Some of us have emptied rivers, eradicated species for this trick of accidental (**LIGHT**).

II.

"When the genial season of the year exercises its influence on the animal, it is said that, yawning, as it were, it opens its shell and so receives a kind of dew, by means of which it becomes impregnated; and that at length it gives (**BIRTH**), after many struggles, to the (**BURDEN**) of its shell, in the shape of pearls, which vary according to the quality of the dew." —Pliny the Elder (*Historia Naturalis*, 9:54)

The Greeks believed that a pearl was made when lightning struck the sea, its surface recalling electric greens and salty curls. Word has it that the Greeks were color-blind. The more longstanding belief was that pearls were raindrops captured and solidified within clams.

Many ages since have been associated with pearl crazes. Unsurprisingly, it was the period of European discovery in the Americas in which the New World became known as the Land of Pearls that first tested the limits of a pearl's ecosystem. When Europe's *Margaritifera margaritifera* mussel could not satiate the European nobility's thirst for solidified raindrops, English pirates preying on Spanish ships likely provided the beads that shuddered from pale earlobes and blinked like so many eyes on velvet cleavage at court. In 1585, Horace Walpole wrote that Queen Elizabeth was at once recognized in her portraits for "a pale roman nose, a vast ruff, a vaster farthingale, and a bushel of pearls" that she'd brought into fashion, though Elizabeth was much later in coming to this (**TREND**) than she may have realized.

(**BIRTH**: Most of the women who spoke with Dr. Stevenson said that violence was the key—the single element from a previous life that made a new body bear old marks, or as Stevenson wrote it, "discarnate personalities influencing a new persona as early as fetal development." Some of the women he spoke with had borne children with maps on their scalps, or moles in cruciform. Long before the phrase "intergenerational trauma" became common, Stevenson posed that that stem cells might recognize emotions. He also thought atoms dispersing in physical human trauma might re-gather themselves in human embryos developing nearby. Or that pregnant women become temporarily extra porous. Like my grandparents, who passed a tumor between them and died two months apart. Or like the stories my family hides most desperately which reliably surface in some other place, and here I'll implicate myself. I'm saying a belief might design a body and not the other way around. I'm saying that the surface of a living container could bear signs of the old lives it contains.)

(**TREND**: Grandma Sarah named my mother after her mother, too. She named her for my great grandmother Margaret, so it's she my mother middle-named me for, and not herself. Having two namesakes seems a lot to carry but, as my father knows, it's also not much to hold as your own.)

(**BURDEN**: The first pearls I owned came in a square, red package that opened on two hinges like a clam, or a book. They weren't round or in a bushel, but they were mine and from my grandmother Sarah who had brought them back from China. My mother named me Sarah after her mother, to keep me for herself. My father had been named for his father and so had "Jr." at the end. Mom hoped my name would save me from inheriting my father's nose bridge and his wandering eye, but a name can only go so far. In her story I was born into a thunderstorm cleaving the summer she had slung me through. Swollen ankles and hot lipstick and sundresses to the ground. My mother says an MBA was what women in the '80s did in case, but by the end of that summer she probably knew some decisions had come too early, and the straight and narrow was coming at her like a two-ton river barge. A generation earlier, my grandmother was standing in a boat on the Mississippi eating fried catfish, wearing gabardine, and sipping her second Manhattan when her water broke. She finished that drink and brought her copy of *War and Peace* to the hospital because she had heard, simply, that the process would be long.)

(**FORGOTTEN**: In my grandma Sarah's past life, she was either her own grandmother or a pearl diver in the Qin Dynasty. Her lifelong friendships with Chinese people and her devotion to art have framed the walls of her home in scrolled mountain ranges that rise in dissonance to the landscape past her curtains. Since the early '80's Sarah has been swimming laps and fostering international relations in Hebei province. She traveled with one of the first American groups to enter China after Mao. At 81, in winter, she still goes down to the small town YMCA each morning to kick wakes that blur the same blue tiles. She'd happily swim in the river she lives beside if it would let her out afterwards. It's from Sarah that I inherited this need to be immersed, to shred a current with five fingers. But the longer I stay out of our river, the less I think of it as a passageway. I like to imagine that Sarah's arms are pruney from years of water rather than loose with age. She has one birthmark above her left elbow that she only shows when she's in her one piece. It's the same birthmark, in the exact same spot, she says, where her own grandmother had a mark. I don't have one there, I checked, tried to make a group of five freckles look like one by squinting. The shared mark could be a sign that Sarah and her grandmother will die in the same manner, that she is her grandmother reincarnate, or that she's approaching a fatal elbow-wound, except that their two lives overlapped like hers and mine do, and though I'm still not clear on the rules, this theory seems to function only in a non-linear conception of time.)

The dew of the Mississippi river is of questionable quality, more questionable than the sweeping, polluted rains that feather its back during August thunderstorms. It would be a long shot to imagine that Iowa's currents still rush with the greatest diversity of freshwater mollusks in the world. Today's Mississippi slides a gritty tongue along the base of cliffs where my grandparents' old house perches in a (**FORGOTTEN**) river town once booming with the freshwater gems pulled from its banks. Today, Muscatine, Iowa, "Pearl of the Mississippi," is trying to revive a historic center of commerce. The cobbled streets between old highbrowed facades flash eerily, barren as the bike racks between empty window displays. Along Muscatine's riverwalk a 40-foot bronze man gripping slender clamming forks is often the lone silhouette beside that waterway—"The Big Muddy," "Ol' Blue," "Father of Waters"— the fast and polluted Mississippi herself, from the Ojibwe ᒥᓯ ᓰᐱᕽ, "Misi-ziibi" or "great river." These are the riverbanks where "explorers" first exchanged greetings and then blows with the Meskwaki who wore freshwater pearls around their necks. Long before they reached Iowa, those white invaders had suspected in the American peoples a kind of fever for nacre suffered by most other human groups on the planet. Today their river is best suited for gazing across.

III.

"We have the impression that, by staying in the motionlessness of its shell, the mollusk is preparing temporal explosions, not to say whirlwinds, of being." —Gaston Bachelard

As early as the third millennium, deep pearl divers in the Persian Gulf, usually enslaved, were combing the seabeds for pearl-bearing oysters to feed a steady market. Their contractors considered the gulf inexhaustible. By the 19th century, standardized pearl boats carried 20 to 30 divers who jumped into the gulf feet first every day, and were pulled rapidly to the bottom by 30-pound stones they retrieved with a rope after resurfacing. The divers were expert breath-holders armed with horn nose-clips, cotton earplugs steeped in oil, and a hip basket for gathering clams in heavy water. Some dove to the bottom repeatedly for as long as daylight lasted.

In the Americas the demand for pearls was so high and the diving so dangerous that in 1520 the (**SUNBURNT**) Spanish enslaved all Lucayans who could plunge as far as eight (**FATHOM**)s during dives (48 feet deeper than most scuba divers will descend with air tanks), and in doing so eradicated a culture in which free divers were also spiritual leaders.

(**SUNBURNT**:
Clouds of mosqui-
tos, and the diseases they
carry, have historically protected some parts of the
Amazon from human
deforestation.)

(**FATHOM**: I'm
not sure if anyone has died
of pearls, and violently, or how, but Lu-
cayan divers perished by drowning. We know they
pushed the limits of lungs trained for generations, and
their baskets were left at the sea bottom. We know the last
pocket of O_2 bloomed out, water poured in, and they floated. For
one taken from their home and forced to repeatedly submerge, a
solitary drowning is a violence. Once, my father came to tuck me in
and found me crying over a boy who had drowned in my book. Maybe
to relate or to give me perspective, he told me the story of his older
brother who had succumbed to croup as a child and had left him
the role of oldest sibling. "Suffocated," he said, and I swallowed.
Unlike my mother, he almost never told old family stories,
secrets that sift generations like recessive alleles. The
kind of stories people only tell to strangers or to
their children (as if those tales could
carry tools inside them).)

(**MERMAID**: My dad's mother, my G-ma, was the best sea-floater this world has seen. She nicknamed herself when I became her first grandchild and she didn't feel grandmotherly yet. She'd earned her own spots in the ocean long before I came, easing a red one-piece across the heights of water soon to be surf. The woman could fall asleep buoyant. She had already middle-named her daughter "Kay" for Kem, the son she lost before my aunt and I were born. My father had never mentioned G-ma's illness until I asked about her yellow pills. G-ma moved like a tide, he explained. She started a prescription, got better, quit it, repeat. "You know how you sometimes feel so high you can stay up for hours working?" my father asked me, "but other times you feel so low it's hard get out of bed? That's what G-ma's like all of the time." As if some genes throb like a collective wound, as if my blood might surge and ebb like hers did. And his. But it's my own mother who taught me that some books are better left unread. She's the family keeper, suspicious and ever-searching. I remember, after my father left us for his nurse, how she spent the night attached to sterile machines that brought her weight back in sour tubes, that forced hydration, and how she seemed unsure of how to touch us afterwards, as if she had been far away and still was. Her friends had known about the other women. So, then she got to be herself with us. Then she got to change. Later, after we moved back to Iowa, a woman who still lived there told her my father had started up with the first woman soon after I was born. And my mother told me she had found pairs of my underwear stuffed into my stepbrother's pillowcase. She said she had hid every photo album my father had made when she knew he would leave us. She read the sexts I sent to my first boyfriend while I was sleeping late on a Saturday. I stay up nights wondering about all that she keeps to herself.)

On the island of Jeju a local saying goes, "Haenyos do the work of the living in the land of the dead."

Sea diving on the South Korean island began as the lowliest of professions, a task considered fitting for women whose fat-lined bodies were thought better suited for diving and retaining heat. Jeju's modern matriarchal culture owes its origins to the first haenyo divers who eared wealth and power in a community where wide hips and seasoned lungs made the breadwinner. Today, the haneyo still pull shells from the depths where their matriarchs have been dodging sharks and men-of-war for centuries. Each diver begins at age 11 and trains for seven years to hold her breath for three full minutes. But their granddaughters are drawn away from the sea by opportunities for education and marriage. So many women have left the profession that in 2003, 85% of the nearly 6,000 registered haenyo divers clawing for abalone 60 feet below the surface were over 50 years old. Today, the last of these "grandmother(**MERMAID**)s" can still be heard sounding a centuries-old whistle from the black surf as they surface with a pale abalone or a beating conch as wide as their head.

IV.

An Iowa folk saying: "No Muscatine resident can enter heaven without evidence of servitude in the (**BUTTON**) industry."

Muscatine's Boepple Button Company, the world's first freshwater pearl button plant, opened its doors to workers in 1891, a full century after Europeans navigated the flat river-flanked land that would become the state of Iowa, 80 years after US treaties erased indigenous rights to the land, and 30 after foundations were laid for the West Second Street house where my mother's family would make their (**HOME**).

John Frederick Boepple had found his way from Hamburg, Germany, to Muscatine with a handful of ideal button-punching shells that he had heard were found in a river 200 miles west of Chicago. He set up his first processing plant along the Mississippi in downtown Muscatine, and within ten years earned the city its folk name by spawning seven pearl button plants that employed half the town's workforce and produced 37% of the world's buttons annually. During Muscatine's equivalent to the gold rush, poor clammer families set up tent and lean-to villages in the pocked, muddy shade of banks where women and children boiled and scraped the mussels that men had plucked from the river's belly.

(**BUTTON**: The first functional pearl buttons I saw out in the world were dotting a western shirt my father wore last Christmas. A self-proclaimed cowboy reincarnate, his ensemble included heeled boots, the kind I'm still not used to on his stout, Southern frame (my own). G-pa, my father's namesake, says he wore pearl-buttoned shirts on racing days when he worked at a horse track as a boy. His buttons were what made a Sunday shirt from a work shirt. Buttons were important because they were for show days when he'd have to stand at the feet of horses having their pictures taken. Long ago, at least one of his buttons, the glint on a horse-tender's good shirt, came from the Pearl City itself.)

(**HOME**: On visitation weekends my our father's anticipation quickly turned to dim surprise. At home our mother constantly discussed him, but my father had designed his new life as if she'd never been a present for it. She'd taken all the furniture, which helped, but it seemed that we still reminded him of a role he'd half-vacated. What he needed was to talk to us directly, but instead he told us "You have a new mom now!" He urged us to unpack, to clean our room. Instead of leaving us at home he brought my sister and I to meetings and on errands, buckling us into the car himself like the small children she had borne him. What he wanted was proximity, so he carried a key to our shared bedroom and used it no matter who yelled "We're changing!" He wanted only to move forward, to be the kind of father not one of us had known.)

(**RIVERBED**: It's hard to imagine the inside of a river—what's in there, how anything knows which way is up. A river that size has several velocities and shifting levels. It has violent undertows, whirlpools, vast ridges and sloughs. After we left Iowa and before we came back, my family's house in Illinois faced a river where someone was always finding a body. Some were dredged up, then into headlines around the holidays, or wound themselves into drainage pipes for teenagers to discover. In third grade I heard a story about someone we knew finding a car rolling along the bottom with a family of five still buckled into its seats. Authorities pulled the car out but no one would touch them. I notice now that a body seems both less human and less like a corpse once it resurfaces from an uninhabitable zone.)

(**PUNCHED**: The year my grandmother Sarah came to visit her friends in the foothills of Tucson, she sat in on the fourth grade poetry class I was teaching downtown. Her eyes traced my path through the sea of small raised hands. Then without losing focus, I watched her reach down and pluck a curling nametag from the dense carpet where it clung after falling from my shirt, and press the tag to her own chest. In evolutionary terms, if we inherit moles as signs of past deaths, is a mole not a tool of natural selection? A means of avoiding learned harms, of narrative defense? What I am saying is that I don't believe in lucky accidents. Especially when it's light or name that comes by chance.)

Iowa clammers of the industrial age were not as keen to dive into murky water for their catch. Instead they stood barefoot in the black mud and in hot metal boats with their pant legs rolled to the knee, dipping crowfoot hooks or clamming forks down to the (**RIVERBED**) to prod tender, open-mouthed mussels that would clamp onto the prongs in defense. These men stood at the banks and on the river late into the evening as fires blinked from the camps on shore. They looked down into the water and up into the bluffs where my grandmother's house sat waiting beneath scores of lightning bugs beating high in the trees.

Mississippi shellfish are named for their shapes and temperaments. heelsplitter and pimpleback, elephant ear, Higgins eye, mapleleaf, pigtoe, pistolgrip, butterfly, black sand, banana, mucket, pocketbook, washboard and ebonyshell. Oblong or wing-shaped, freckled and palomino, their shells were splashed in black and purple swatches beneath skins of river mud. The best shells were wide, flat as the land and of uniform thickness. Once (**PUNCHED**) clean of disks, the shells resembled thin slices of honeycomb and were crushed and churned into cement to pave the roads in a town where I pulled rainbow shards from potholes as a kid. In the factories, loose shell meat was occasionally used as hog feed or stirred back into the land as fertilizer, but often the shellfish were dumped, boneless, back into the river they'd grown inside for a decade.

V.

Iowa's famous skyline features golden rows receding to unmarred forever, the soybean patch topped by a roosterish barn, like the postcard landscapes from the era between Ag and Big Ag, before plows field-paved all but 10% of our state's natural (**HABITAT**) and family farms became endangered. That great hunger for acreage has become our own for meat and animal feed, and together we've made Iowa's the most altered landscape in the nation, and not simply because the place is flat—that helped. Industrial agriculture is in Iowa because its soil was once the most coveted in the world. The earth there was famously black and still is, if you dig deep enough, because Iowa's was once a soggy terrain netted by many (**ROOTS**) that held water like a woven mat. It was mostly wetlands and marshes, forests and prairies that blazed and rose from ash and were smothered by snow in our longest season. Diverse birds thrived there and were digested or died in accordance in the marshes where they steeped and blackened to raise the next prairie.

Then for two decades our river was thick with felled pines. We drained the marshes for fields. Today we open the oldest acres with steel combines to plant monocrops each year. That singular modified vegetation draws out the same brand of nutrients so that each season Iowa's soil gets grittier and more sand-colored and we need to keep digging. Our automated irrigators funnel waterways into fields. The topsoil skims off and runs into ditches, trailing pesticide and fertilizer. It sifts into creeks and canals and slowly, eventually, it finds the darkening river where the spent earth rains diagonally to lay a bed for shellfish long gone.

(**HABITAT**: Most rivers today are the dead kind. The shipping kind. The fish bad to eat. This shift in contents alters the way people conceive of waterways as integral to landscape, what they pull out and are willing to put into it, and what their children become alongside, as if that mattered to a shellfish. A river with no mussels to sing its name has forgotten itself. A shell is an exoskeleton as well as a self and a house—this is the thing they punched pieces from. For a river to be reincarnated would mean the river itself could die, but even fish can't breathe water. Button-makers left dark circles that marked a violent end—the type of death, some say, a mole can recall.)

(**ROOTS**: Have you ever wondered about wild species that thrive in farmed landscape? Or imagined there are rare mussels in the Mississippi River despite the dredging that gnaws at their home? Farm fertilizer gets into the water and breeds algae skins that block out sun. The black earth and its liquids get reshuffled and sickly combined. My grandmother serves on every new conservation board, riverwalk committee, and short-lived rejuvenation project in town. This year it's "Brews and Bees." And my grandfather once headed the Iowa Department of Natural Resources before he quit during a disagreement about legalizing lead ammunition for Iowa dove hunters. Together they act as vertices of this space in and around the river, negotiating at its boundaries, holding shaky ground. Together they raise generations of demonic velvet-black dogs, bred for hunting birds. The newest one is named Pearl, like my mother, Margaret—from Margarita, the Greco-Roman word for pearl, daughter of a Sarah, mother of pearls, who had no idea she'd named her daughter and her dog the same.)

(**SECRETS**: A
book is a way to think. I
became a difficult teenager with
a misdemeanor, a temper, and heavy
piercings in cartilaginous zones. My mother
encouraged me to quiet down, to learn to rely
on myself because one day, she said, everyone
I knew would desert me. None of them could
help it. "Even me," she explained, "but," she
pointed to my piercings encouragingly,
"there's more here than meets
the eye.")

(**WOUND**:
That would have
made a nasty birth-
mark.)

(**SWALLOWED**: Once, I
died in a river. I died as the river
did. Unlikely waters polluted my interior
and I bled into myself and didn't sink. I was the
gas and I was the spitball tumor growing solid in
a crevice. I was the stuff a breathing body houses in
other containers. I was the fat of a pistolgrip, a heelsplitter pulled from its bones and I was a black land with
no mountain to halt the plow. The drowning response
is noiseless and confined to subtle movements. I
flailed as I could. I went quiet in a matter of
two minutes and along my right flank,
below 13 moles, broken vessels
swayed in water.)

Back in button times, John Boepple was the first to notice signs of over-harvesting in the newly barren waters around Muscatine. He perfected his version of the crowfoot hook, which stopped injured mussels from falling off, and captured the biggest ones, leaving young shells to grow before picking. Boepple was an old-world man, suspicious and poorly suited for business. He ordered unusual equipment to baffle competitors who he was sure were trying to steal his button (**SECRETS**). In 1910 he quit buttons for a job at the Fairport Biological Station to study mussel populations as Iowa's natural habitats were starting to be dredged and plowed, driven and sequestered to the banks. In the same year, legend has it that Boepple stepped on a mussel while working in a river and died the following year in Muscatine of a blood infection from the (**WOUND**).

By 1957, plastics had almost replaced pearl buttons and took most of Muscatine's jobs with them. In warehouses along the Mississippi, machines poured polyester syrup into flat, white sheets and punched fit or blanks that made cheap, flexible buttons in a fraction of the time. Plastics floating downstream on the surface of the water, sinking to its belly, sticking to its dams. The same material in faux pearls sold as cheap nacre in shopping malls. Many of Muscatine's smaller factories switched to plastic production for a time, but most were bought out by larger companies as button business moved to bigger cities. The last of the old button plants in Muscatine today still manufactures plastic products for packaging and electronics, the bits that can be (**SWALLOWED**) by toddlers but never recycled.

HANDLING THE BEAST

8,000 BCE, THE BLACK PÉRIGORD OF SOUTHWESTERN FRANCE:

A cave system is forming. At the end of the last ice age, water seeps into fissures in the high cliffs along the Vézère River. What begins as the slow drip of melting glacier soon becomes a subterranean river that carefully slices 250 meters of branching passages within the limestone bluff, opening what will later be known as La Grotte de Lascaux. The extensive cave paintings preserved within show that early *Homo sapiens* crept inside by widening the entrance to this grotto during the Upper Paleolithic period and used the protected walls of its interior not for shelter, but as canvas upon which to create the first art we recognize.

(Of the 400 figures depicted at Lascaux, only one is anthropomorphic. One semi-human figure with a bird-like head rests, angular, perhaps fallen, before an eviscerated bull with innards dangling from its open belly. Human figures are rare in cave art from this period. When they exist, their bodies are disguised with wild appendages and rendered roughly as compared to their non-human counterparts. The legacy those first conscious beings left is not one of texts, tools, or architectures, but representations of the wildness outside of them. The Italian theorist Giorgio Agamben has since written that "the human-animal divide" has since been a way of dividing the human from itself. Some prehistorians theorize that the Lascaux paintings reflect how, in the first moment humans developed a certain grey matter they also recognized how they were different, and drew other creatures repetitively as their first expression of mankind's loneliness, a consideration of that distance, of the animal they still recognized inside themselves, a nostalgia for earlier days.) At the moment they hopped the crevice spanning the animal and human brain, cave artists began to create art that grappled with "the beasts they had been."

1869 CE, THE FRENCH CARIBBEAN:

Aesop's fables are being translated into Creole. Through volumes like *Fables Créoles Dédiées aux Dames de l'île Bourbon* (Creole Fables for Island Women), colonists in the Seychelles are impressing French culture upon native island peoples via literature. Most of the stories are *beast fables* or *beast epics*, short stories or poems in which animals speak and human behavior is subject to scrutiny by reflection on the animal kingdom. Beast fables were passed down in oral tradition long before Aesop's recording of them. They precede and likely inform the bestiaries of medieval Europe, illustrated volumes describing various real and mythical animals that served as symbols in the visual language of Christian art of the period. Bestiaries became beast epics related to religious teachings, a cataloguing of animals and the ways humans could learn from their example.

(One of the main benefits of bipedalism was its freeing the hands for activities other than forward motion. The Neanderthal could plod upright, bowlegged, could raise a high flame, craft hand tools, bury her dead—but she did not, as far as we know, leave any record of representational art. With a sharp blooming in her species' cranial capacity came the advent of a "creative explosion" that marks the birth of *Homo sapiens*, the first artists, and their newly vast imaginations. It was *Homo sapiens* who pressed five toes into the Dordogne River sand, a burier of grave goods and a self-adorner, who hunted for manganese to grind into pigment for art alone.)

157 CE, BERGAMA, TURKEY:

Galen of Pergamon eviscerates an ape before the High Priest of Asia. He then mends the damage to the primate's body, winning himself the post of physician to the priest's gladiators, men hired to battle the formidable animals called beasts after being brought to Bergama from lesser-known corners of the continent. Both men and beasts were kept in cells of the stone corridors below the floor of massive arenas where Galen sometimes worked. Ever the student, Galen referred to the wounds of his patients as "windows into the body." Following his post as physician, Galen became one of the most prominent researchers of antiquity. He performed countless dissections, primarily of the tissues of the Barbary ape. Galen produced the first drawings of the inner musculature of an ape's hand, which contains all of the structures present in humans, differing only in the tapering of the ape's slender wrist and fingertips, and in the proportional development of muscles rendering the ape's thumb only partially opposable. As the grandfather of western medicine, his drawings served as models for the crude surgical processes of many ages that followed.

(When one studies the figures at Lascaux, it becomes clear that the natural formation of the cave wall was a primary influence for a figure's placement upon it. Often, an existing rock shelf became the ground on which a painted herd ran, a sharp cleft gave dimension to the tucked neck of an equine. We can imagine the earliest human artists planning their work the way their descendants would in millennia to come, by grazing palms along the inner rock faces, tracing grooves with fingertips in search of spines, a sinuous flank. When the first artists traced pigments to stone, it was not their own likeness, but those likenesses of the creatures around them that they drew. These animal figures were layered, stacked in lines or packs suggesting procession or stampede. They were dusted with pattern, empty to suggest whiteness, heavy bellied, bent. None were captured in stillness. These first attempts at representation proved detailed enough that humans living 35,000 years later could identify and catalogue 605 of the 900 depicted species, and counting.)

1994 CE, OUTSIDE MONTIGNAC, FRANCE:

I step across a threshold of limestone into the slick chill of French subterrane. My damp palm is wrapped in my mother's long fingers. A hard pool of sunlight at the entrance quickly fades as we descend further into the rock face and my mother ducks her forehead down towards mine. I let her lead me forward blindly and tilt my head back to gaze beyond the brim of my sun hat where flat figures are streaming slowly overhead. *Faites attention*, she warns, practicing our French. Our flashlights skip across the sharp ceilings in a flickering that recalls torch light, that stretches and plucks at those painted skins until I am sure they are tugging across the rock in the darkness, swimming beneath. I remember wondering how the images had been placed there and why we didn't just take them back out into the light with us. I remember guessing that we had shuffled miles into the dark, that the black passages opening in the swoop of yellow beams were endlessly descending into the earth.

(The musculature of a hand cannot be dissected without a hand. Nor can its tunnels and crevices be detailed and recorded without the precise wielding of a pen. Thirty-five thousand years before Galen of Pergamon pressed fingerprint to fingerprint, split the skin, Paleolithic artists and dissectors of southern France commanded the same manual precision in their own renderings, in their excavations of anatomy. We know this because they left finger bones behind. Today, we can guess at the contours of flesh that once encased the marrow of those artists through the study of similar existing species. The recorded curve of earliest human musculature presents itself to us only in handprints stenciled on the walls of Lascaux. To create these distinct marks, early artists blew crushed pigment directly from their mouth onto the bare stone between their five spread fingers, a signature, a symbol of their existing at all.)

2007 CE, IOWA CITY, USA:

My mother is chewing her cuticles. They are shining, raw down to the first knuckle around nails she leaves beautiful, intact. With me away at school her nerves are singing at a higher frequency. I took with me a part of the order she imposed upon our days. *Faites attention*, I warn into the phone. I lay in a lofted bed, and imagine I possess a kind of psychic power to ease anxieties—those that, like my mother's, slept inside me until adulthood. I imagine that I can conjure freeze-frame images of the people I love in whatever exact motion they are making. Like a long-distance x-ray. With this ability, I might check to see if they assume positions of comfort, or attitudes that require attention. Maybe this seemed less invasive than calling for the fourth time. Or rather more plausible, like the universe would only grant me this specific skill. If it did, I could squeeze my eyes shut in the dark to see my mother curled C-wise in her bed, or with skull cradled in palms. What worried me most were the forms I couldn't imagine, positions that pained her, those I never knew. Lying there, I pictured her outline reading in a chair or laughing in TV glow, and I'd then find sleep.

(Some theorists concerned with the intent behind the paintings at Lascaux pose that the animal figures there are acts of "sympathetic magic," early humans' attempt to influence reality through representation, the way contemporary practitioners of Voodoo still do. This theory suggests that the Paleolithic hunter made his first kill on the walls of Lascaux to prompt the kill incarnate to present itself on the hunt. Others have suggested that, as at similar sites, the symbols placed upon the body of the drawn animal detail effective wound placement—that the first art recorded and instructed in successful killing techniques. Each drawing marks an expression of early human desire, that together the figures display a chorus of individual hopeful voices, of unique signatures moving together in a pack.)

1940 CE, OUTSIDE MONTIGNAC, FRANCE:

A village myth: A small dog named Robot wanders away near the Vézère River. He leads four teenage boys to the mouth of a cave where perhaps no human foot has padded for tens of thousands of years. "We have learnt nothing!" exclaimed an exasperated Picasso upon his visit to Lascaux the year of its discovery. This encounter would have been especially unnerving for the cofounder of cubism who favored bulls both as a child and in his best-known works as an adult. The paintings were also unusually similar to the thick black outlining favored by Picasso and his contemporaries who were nicknamed les fauves, the wild ones. The bulls there are actually the aurochs, an extinct species of oxen. The site's Great Black Bull panel, a 17-foot aurochs, is the largest animal painting ever discovered in cave art. Long after its first rendering, the aurochs served as a vital game animal and attained mythic significance for numerous cultures. Like domestic cattle, the aurochs carried a cross-shaped bone in its heart, believed to be a sign of its magical powers.

(The figures at Lascaux present a unique puzzle for modern visitors and historians. They are singular, but overlapping. Differing species are placed in procession alongside one another. Some decorated panels contain only one very small or large figure; others hold many. Because two entrances once existed, it is difficult to discern in which order the paintings are intended to progress. Though fossil records of the Périgord show that the animals depicted there lived in the cave's vicinity, by no means are all species accounted for upon its walls. Initially, finding no clear patterns in their rendering, historians entertained the theory that the paintings at Lascaux were created as doodles, as art for art's sake.)

1900 CE, THE CAVE OF MAS D'AZIL, THE SOUTHERN FRENCH PYRENEES:

In the deep corners of a cave through which a highway will someday run, French explorers discover the skull of a young girl with her teeth removed, with circular reindeer vertebrae set within her empty eye sockets. They find a reindeer horn carved with three detailed horse heads. The first carved head depicts an intact equine head, its flared nostrils clearly delineated, the second shows a head stripped of most tissue, its skull deeply shadowed, the third head has been lightly skinned, so that the contours of the surface muscles can be detailed. These carvings reveal that the early human artists were curious about the inner parts of creatures, about how life, as emergence, resulted in the combination of similar physical structures, and was absent in their separation.

(The cave paintings at Lascaux are read as a kind of bestiary by prehistorians who understand each species as a symbol or allegory, like hieroglyphics, like an alphabet, like pixels. Each animal there is linked associatively to form our most ancient recorded narrative spanning the entire cave system.)

2009 CE, OUTSIDE MINNEAPOLIS, USA:

I sit tucked into a corner of level 3½ at Rolvaag Library studying art history. My hands rest, clawlike in LCD light, as 17,000-year-old paintings float across my screen to eerie music via an official French website. Lascaux was first closed to visitors in 2008, during attempts to battle a black fungus that began to crawl across the walls after the introduction of AC and 1,200 daily breathers and their bacteria. This year, it was closed indefinitely. The entrance was locked and a replica cave was buried 200 meters away. Cross-legged, I am studying the earliest example of art in the only way a human can these days—via replication. From here I can consider the paintings up close. Evidence of alterations and edits are visible in the aging of a stag's pigment. Extinct felines lurk in low profile in the darkest corners of the painted world, as they did in life. Scattered among them rest slender hook and arrow patterns. Missing entirely are representations of the cliffs or river. The theories behind the paintings are contradictory, impossible to enumerate. Few can agree on even basic interpretations, and I feel no inclination to choose.

(The aurochs, after stags and equines, are the species most numerous in Lascaux imagery. Absent from the paintings are reindeer, which prehistorians believe to be the primary food source of the local artists. To these researchers, the creatures the upper Paleolithic artists chose to represent were those formidable in size or capabilities, those they feared or interacted with closely but did not consume, the beasts they respected, those they thought a match for their new minds.)

2019 CE, CLEVELAND, USA:

I break my hand falling down the stairs, carrying a stack of books. Deep in the palm, the fifth metacarpal is no longer called the "pinky." The doctor calls it a "boxer's injury." "But more like a brawler's," he says. Hand vs. books vs. stairs. I won't be handwriting or typing for two months. In my bedroom time moves slowly. A black-eyed cat is hypnotized by the ceiling fan and my right foot is hurting—fifth metacarpal—a phantom ache in the twin bone that, eons ago, had the potential to become a finger.

(Two existing photographs taken a decade apart capture Pablo Picasso wearing a bull head mask. One was taken for the cover of *LIFE* magazine and the other by Edward Quinn. In each photograph, Picasso is bare chested and gesturing with his arms. Some have speculated that the mask is a reference to Picasso's Spanish heritage and the country's association with bullfights, while others suggest that the hybrid portrait references the presence of the bull as a symbol throughout his work. Some say that in his work the bull always serves as a kind of self-portrait.)

2012 CE, TUCSON, USA:

Onscreen, a small Black girl stands inches from a massive bovine whose nostrils stare back into her eyes. Earlier in the film *Beasts of the Southern Wild*, children living in the mythical Bathtub, a piece of land below sea level mirroring coastal Louisiana, are warned by their Creole teacher of the coming of the terrible aurochs. This teacher, who bears an aurochs tattoo upon her thigh, describes to the children a boar-like beast that consumes humans and will soon be freed from the melting icecaps in which it was imprisoned during the ice age. In one scene, the protagonist, Hushpuppy, climbs inside a cardboard box as her home burns down and records her life on its inner walls. She wonders, "How're people going to look back on my civilization?" Later, Hushpuppy's father instructs her in survival techniques by encouraging her to crack a crab shell without the use of a knife, to lure a catfish with her tiny wiggling fingers, to pluck it from the water just as it clasps hard above her knuckle.

(In *Beasts*, the aurochs is painted as an apocalyptic animal, a predator accompanying disaster that serves as a symbol for a number of narrative themes. Among them: evolution, extinction, violence against Black people, and the human grappling with the order of the cosmos. This twentieth-century film echoes themes which earlier prehistorians saw in connecting biological behavior to cosmic patterns at Lascaux. In these theories, the real aurochs processing in lines among other painted species symbolized the progression of seasons and, alongside other beasts, represented the rhythm and circular, regenerative cycles of nature and time. Early artists were perhaps the first beings to contemplate natural systems, those widest parts of the cosmos we still do not fully comprehend. Art then served as these creatures' first method of ordering the world, of articulating their newly complex human fears and desires. They drew what they were decidedly not—the creatures they had last been. They pointed at the line between and toed back across it. They engaged in just what their new minds were built for—in shuffling, making meaning from component parts.)

NEST

((

Once, in late summer, on a small island in Lake Ontario, I climbed ten feet to build a nest in a birch tree. I was ten and mine was the tallest tree growing there, a quarter mile offshore from my grandfather's hunting cabin, but not an especially tall tree since the island was mostly a rocky shoreline where a fire had raged years before. Loons built their nests somewhere in the reeds. We saw their silhouettes knifing into the lake on nights when the moon was out. Like them I was in shouting distance of the cabin I had canoed away from but feeling very wild and alone indeed, nailing planks to a tree where my own nest would swoon above the water (It would be many years until I saw a ground nest—hundreds of them actually—together in a colony on a very different island in the Sea of Cortez. From a distance that island looked shadowed and grey, but as our boat sped closer it became obvious that the landform was coated entirely in white by generations of birds evacuating their bowels over its short peaks. I mean it was encrusted—fully powdered in dried shit. That island earned its name in the same way the better-known Alcatraz had, from the alcatraces, *strange birds* seen there in droves by locals. By the time we arrived, the place was inhabited only by nesting seabirds known to collectively attack if disturbed, and we were warned at length not to approach them ((A girl I went to college with once built a human-sized ground nest for a show at which I displayed a series of terrible watercolors involving cocoons. I truly wanted to sit inside her nest, which was lined with fleece blankets—the kind White-Anglo-Saxon-Protestants order monogrammed with custom initials from Land's End—but I could not sit in the nest because this girl was no longer my friend, because during sophomore year she had made everyone start calling her by her new artist's name and I wouldn't do it. In the beginning I sometimes forgot to but after a while it became a thing I did on purpose and this of course made the girl upset. Still I might have known better. We were far from home and in the early window when a person has a chance to become more familiar to herself. We were thinking about women artists like Kiki Smith and Marina Abramović, we were celebrating "Chicago." Now I know more, but back then I rejected the idea of an "artist's name" at all maybe for art reasons maybe for reasons of circumstance, or maybe because each of us had a been given a biblical name and attended a Scandinavian college full of white girls, and I felt like we all had to face that. Like it was wrong to ask others to make you feel unusual rather than part of a collective, average and flabby all at once. I had never seen so many people just like me. And then there were my ugly cocoons (((The term *flap* was a verb among the words that, for too long, I believed originated in my family's dialect and made us peculiar.

Like *smarmy* and *biscuit*, *flap* occurred with a frequency shifting it into something idiosyncratic that I thought belonged to us alone. If you don't know already, *flapping* describes the act of grabbing a blanket by neighboring corners and flicking it open across a person who is lying down so that the air moves across them as from a wing being beaten and the blanket falls perfectly flat. *Flapping* is a tucking-in-without-the-tuck that results in the ideal, total blanket encasement up to the neck with just the head left uncovered to watch for monsters or simply breathe easy in sleep. One cannot flap oneself—this is important ((((There is something conceptual about encasement that humans are pulled to reproduce—something beyond swaddling that has to do with a nest. For me, the nest is cliché and precious, a form that should be over by now. The interesting thing about the nest is a characteristic Frank Lloyd Wright made famous in his residential designs—an element called "prospect and refuge," the contrast of a snug bed with an open vista. It is the chime of security and freedom together, not to mention a view, that our genetic memory calls for. Something now enjoyed in its extremity by only the most isolated and well-off (((((But designer Janine Benyus, known for her work in biomimicry, says that the thing about nest places is the shapes the light makes coming through branches there. Benyus says that because humans were tree-dwellers a millennium ago, we evolved under a set of fractal shadow patterns ((((((Which means a structure composed of identical shapes at every scale. Like the golden ratio, a fractal is a perfect mathematical set occurring in nature. Fractals work like nested dolls—they self-reference internally. Think the center of a mandala expanding. Number the fern leaves that narrow to each point. When magnified, a fractal pattern should contain minute versions of its larger self. Natural forms are often fractal because their sequences duplicate to produce growth. The shapes of estuaries, of lightning, seashells, and the clustering of bird nests in some colonies form these designs. The weave structure of a nest is often fractal too. Human lungs are dendric, tree-like at every magnification because of the exact subdivisions of air and chambers within (((((((nest patterns into us ((((((((nestle ( ) divide)))))))) into nest patterns))))))). And the architecture of our neuron channels—fractal, ascending. Their patterns stack to form the layered web that serves our brain and all its distant connections)))))). Something within us sees these branch-light patterns as signals of safety, or home, and Benyus argues that we evolved to visually prefer architecture that contains such structures))))).

So the great apes make nests. As do Marina Abramović, Porky Hefer, and Patrick Dougherty. Jason Flynn has a human-sized weaverbird nest at

Big Sur that is lined with down blankets and goes for $110 a night. Anthropologie sells a nest-chair for $10,000 to people who wish to roost inside their homes. And backstage at school, I once made a nest of costumes and hid out when I forgot my lines during "On Being Wright," a play in which I was cast as Frank's French teacher. In common speech a nest can be the place where evil resides. It's a real and metaphoric harbor for snakes and spiders and hornets, for creatures easily enraged. The nest is also the symbolic host to traditional divisions of inner and outer, mine and yours; its very function is based on life-death relationships that depend entirely on who built the nest we speak of; it's not that the nest is a perfect structure, or a beautiful one, but a boundary—one exacted by eons of builders, trying and erring in the name of safety, stacking and weaving among trees, repeat)))).   My father had perfected the flapping motion, but was rarely around to perform it at bedtime. When he was, he would give me a bath and wrap me in a white towel that came down to my ankles. Then he'd let me hide in my room before he came in, growling like a monster, to grab me from where I was hiding. I would stash myself in the bedcovers, flattening my body so that he couldn't see me down in between them until one night I made a decoy nest with my wet towel between the sheets and I hid under the bed without anything on. I watched my father come in all monster-walk-like and snatch the bundle from the bed before freezing and going silent and then ducking his head beneath the frame to discover and tickle me for tricking him. My mother never participated in our routine, so when he left I stopped seeing monsters and ever being flapped))).   But anyway, this girl's nest was pretty special and well-made, even if it was during a time when my girlfriends who were artists were making work under other women's names. I still couldn't sit in it even though she stood there not making eye contact with me or my egregious watercolors, even though we hadn't been friends for a very long time because now she ran with a newer crowd of better artists and she had once told another girl that she didn't respect me as a woman anymore, and that stuck with me, though it would take me a long time to understand what it meant)).   On Alcatraz, bits of tide wrack dotted the beach between whole and partial bird carcasses, salt-eaten bones, some with flesh still draped from their armature. Most were tangled in fishing nets or missing a head. I could see over and into the grasses where white gulls and cormorants were roosting in old and new nests that nearly touched—cups woven from the dried grasses that surrounded. Some had egg-blue fibers from boat ropes and others involved the wing feathers of larger birds rotting on the beach. Soft things are scarce on the coastline, so seabirds sometimes tear apart one another's nests for materials. This is especially brutal if we consider that a bird's nest is a surrogate womb. An organ-like basket; soft to cup and keep the heat therein. The advantage of a ground nest is trustworthy neighbors, shelter from wind, a view of the sky, and that it is impossible to fall from. But because of its disadvantages, humans never nested on the ground).

In my family, the story of that island in Ontario goes like this: When my mother was in hard labor, it was a view of this island she imagined when the doctor suggested she try to visualize something to calm her body down. Now my family has this ritual of looking out to the water and trying to say something about a place we can't explain. Sometimes my mother says she imagined the sky behind the island russet and flushed, and other times a clear blue the way it was when I held a board to the white bark there a decade later and stepped up to nail another high above the lake, to a place where someday, raccoons would clamber and leave empty crayfish, where my iron nails would poison and fell the tree we had loved for two generations. But that afternoon I leaned into the trunk with an armful of nesting, hitching up past the wider branches, the trunk thinning as I climbed—it was a young tree and bending—so when the sixth plank broke beneath my weight I let go of what I carried and the next thing I remember is the breath knocked from me and a view of clouds through leaves. I turned an ear to the ground between two stumps still charred and rooted to the island. Across the lake was the hunting cabin, where there were no witnesses at all.

FOUL CHUTES: ON THE ARCHIVE DOWNRIVER

~

The house was exactly one hundred years older than my sister. It stood facing the river across from another white house where, in 1932, the LaRosa family installed the first laundry chute in Rockford, Illinois, long before our city was named the country's "third most miserable." By the mid-'90s a highway ran between my family's ailing Victorian and its Mississippi tributary and for ten years we lived up there, where Brown's Road ended, where the street might have tipped over the hill and rushed across the stinking river if someone hadn't changed his mind. We wore kitchen-scissor bangs and liked to hang out at the dead end beside our porch—a bald gully stained with mulberries where we played at being orphaned, though we were far from it—past the broken curb where lost cars drew circles in the gravel. We preferred the dead end to our yard because it collected street trash and there we could sort out the best of it.

In June of 1998, while he was renovating his home in St. Louis, Joseph Heathcott discovered a collection of trash in the cavity between his pantry and his laundry chute. It was a stack of paper scraps with sooty edges that were just beginning to stick and combine. There was a box of playing cards, a train ticket from Kansas, a receipt, a diary entry, and a laundry ticket. In "Reading the Accidental Archive," Heathcott wrote that from these materials he could read the tensions between the upward motivations and the limits to mobility of the early middle-class families just four miles from the Mississippi.

~

As still happens in much of the world, the first method of washing clothes in colonial America was at the riverbank.

~

MINNESOTA

My best friend Meg steadies her knee to make a step-up for

my hiking boot. "Let's not get lost now," she says, the words tight with instant coffee and transgression. She looks past her shoulder into rural Mississippi and tips my bottom half over the chain link. I land askew, past the fence on a beveled slab of concrete that starts ringing hollowly. The sky is netted with branches; cold cement stretches out on either side. A little blood starts to pill at my kneecap as I sit up in what looks like the bowl of a babydoll-sized skate park. Its gray half-pipes rise no higher than my knees and dip irregularly along the rims. They make the same bizarre, undulating shape I've been tracing on my laptop screen for months. When I stand and follow the shape into the brush, the bowl balloons wider, like an amoeba. It takes three steps to walk into the rest of the abandoned Mississippi River Model, a miniature version of the watershed that the US Army Corps carved and abandoned here, outside Jackson, 70 years ago, and now Meg and I are officially trespassing.

~

If a river is the lifeline crease at the center of a hand, then a watershed is the palm and five fingers extending; it is impossible to describe the first phenomenon without the rest. A watershed funnels snowmelt on a slight decline. Before the river becomes a river, it is water threading wheat furrows, filling lots and flushing

Cartographer and artist Denis Wood defines "shadowed spaces," as necessary places of refuge for deviant acts within every culture. Deviant acts, as Wood defines them, include a variety of common behaviors—everything from general "hanky-panky," to voting for the villainous party, to dumping toxic waste—similar only in that someone would prefer to keep each one hidden. Wood's shadowed spaces are edge areas "that thrive in the bottom of unworked quarries: they're the spaces underneath the bridges, spotted with guano. . . ."

~

In 1895, the *New York Times* reported that a janitor had discovered a small human skull near the opening to the chute in a West 46th Street tenement house. The writer noted that the skull had "evidently been boiled at some time" and was believed to belong to Susie Martin, who had gone missing when her mother sent her out to gather coal, and whose

alleys before making its way, in many small batches, all the way down to a bank. When the river floods it ruins a city by erasing its edges—those barriers set up between the sewer and the roadway, the pasture and the school yard, a city's dump and its downtown market. A watershed makes lived spaces look, occasionally, in newspapers and on television, as if they were stewing in the river.

body had been found near West 39th Street a few days after her disappearance, without its head.

~

~

WISCONSIN

In 1927, a long time before Meg and I drove together to Mississippi, after months of heavy snowfall that was followed by rain in Minnesota and Wisconsin, the Mississippi River flooded its watershed for 23,000 square miles. Every city with enough money had built levees, directing more water towards the main channels. But a decade earlier the lumber barons had cut away the great forests lining the banks, and industrial farming had drained the prairies, which for centuries had functioned like a sponge for river water. Without the root systems to trap it the floodwaters spread across the plains,

Among the oppressive qualities of suburbs, I've noticed that there are very few undomestic places where anything can take place out of sight. "Nothing disposes easily anymore," writes urban planner Kevin Lynch, "our old poisons return to us." In the mid-'70s, Lynch observed that modern suburbs were lacking in waste spaces. Lynch also encouraged the reclamation of derelict areas like rail yards, cattle grounds, and floodplains—the places, he argued, that would become essential once vacancy was a thing of the past.

~

In the summer of 1999, during the Tate Thames Dig, volunteers collected

scouring fields, reshaping valleys, and surrounding great hills where lone houses stood that would survive and someday be ours. Herbert Hoover called it "the greatest peacetime calamity" in America's history. That calamity inspired the Flood Control Act of '28, which called on the Army Corps of Engineers to "de-fend" America's citizens against their most central waterway. The Army Corps first real solution would be a scale model of the entire Mississippi watershed built on 200 acres, a portion of the real watershed, outside Jackson, Mississippi.

materials along the banks of the river Thames, at low tide, near the Tate Gallery. The objects they found dated from as far back as the medieval period and as recently as that same year. They displayed items from this collection with care and reverence in a mahogany cabinet at the Tate until 2000. That year, a critic wrote that the Thames "can be considered to be a museum, containing a collection [. . .] sorted and classified according to the river's own internal physical dynamics. The nature of the river as a continuum is reflected in the undifferentiated material."

When Albert Einstein's oldest son Hans had said that he wanted to study the movements of river water, Einstein asked him why he wanted to pursue something so difficult. And every time the US Army Corps built a new levee along the Mississippi, they flooded a city further down. Major Eugene Reybold saw their trial-and-error tactics approaching Memphis, and he suggested they try thinking of the river as a system rather than individual limbs. Soon the headlines reported "the colossal effigy of Old

The first laundry chutes turn up in American newspapers and advertisements around 1880, an era that Mira Engler, "scholar of rejected landscapes," has called the time of "Diverting Waste to the Public." Engler says this era is marked by the early control of waste due to major discoveries that, at long last, linked waste to the spread of disease via pathogens too small for doctors to see with naked eyes. Florence Nightingale had already encouraged divisions in public hospitals that moved used linens away from areas designated for caregiving. She argued that laundry should

Man River," being built just outside of Jackson, where the Corps planned to "make little floods to help America protect herself against big ones," to tame "the mighty dragon that is the Mississippi." Their model condensed all 1.4 million square miles of the watershed into 200 acres. It took 23 years to complete. In bird's-eye photographs from the '50s, the model river looks like a root system carved in relief, its empty tendrils dividing the blunted brush. When the Army Corps flushed it with water, the model's tests predicted floods on the real Mississippi River to a matter of inches. But they took too long to finish, and just seven years after the model was complete its outbuildings, pumps, and paperwork were left to rot in Jackson in favor of digital models that could predict floods about half as accurately, but without a staff of engineers.

never be processed near vulnerable patients. "Nothing answers so well as foul-linen shoots," Nightingale wrote, "These should be built in the wall. The best material for them is glazed earthenware piping that can be flushed with water." In the very same era, Midwestern newspapers and farming journals ran campaigns for the drainage of "malarial wetlands" to create the miracle of brand-new farmland—a landscape that no longer absorbed water—and newly relating ideas about productive land and waste.

~

~

A week before spring break I booked the last room in Jackson, drove to Tennessee, and talked Meg into driving 12 more hours in gray weather to walk around an eight-mile gutter. Our friendship, built across trips like this one, began when one of us convinced the other to skip a class or a shift and on every occasion we both wound up deeply carsick. I always thought talking was easier in the car, but Meg preferred the quiet and the view. I drove. In Memphis she took a turn at the wheel and described that September, when she'd dated first a roadie and then a rhetorician and got ordained on her back

Denis Wood wrote "Shadowed Spaces" as a response to Michael Sorkin's *Indefensible Space*, a book that examined American anxiety following increased surveillance after 9/11. But Wood really started writing about shadowed space because he was curious about certain objects that wound up in unsurveilled places. "Once you start

porch while holding a breakfast burrito and a joint. Two hours outside Jackson the western sky bruised itself green and then peach, and I heard tornado sirens for the first time since I was a kid. Our hotel was dressed like a midgrade hunting lodge with maple leaf carpet and a free cocktail hour—no whiskey, no limes. We took lemons and joined a set of Jesuits and a State Highway Patrol conference near the gas fire. The next morning we shared oversweet muffins with the business casuals and open carries. We crossed city limits in boots and neon tights.

~

Some say the earliest laundry chutes were fabric sleeves threaded between floors. Today a laundry chute is the open throat of an old house. Children are drawn to chutes because they invite fantastic dangers (like falling through the home), as well as the taboos attached to personal stains. The apartment where I live has a linen chute that has long been painted shut, but I can press my ear against it to learn if the dryer in the basement is done. I hear a rushing sound in the chute even after the dark drum quits spinning—my ear a dry seashell sounding the tides of the house.

~

looking for them, you find them all the time," Wood writes, "Discarded underpants: white jockey shorts, about size 32. Jockey shorts exclusively. Invariably white. Never smaller than a 26, rarely larger than a 34." What truly inspired Denis Wood was his interest in lost underwear.

~

In 1916, the *New York Herald* reported that a patient at the Magdalen Asylum had slid "at a scorching speed" down a laundry chute that was 90 feet long and 24 inches wide. Women were sent to the Magdalen Asylum for behaviors like drinking and prostitution. Poor conditions there often drove patients to riot and throw themselves from windows into the neighboring quarry. Before 1916,

I'm alone in the model with a skinned knee and Meg is calling down through the brush: "Baby girl? I can't see you!" She follows my head along the chain link until she finds a weak spot. I sit back on my heels and trace the bright moss lining a divot that would stretch a mile at full scale. Meg slides from the bank into the chilly shade. "Whoa," she says slowly. From this vantage the dried-out river model looks like a sci-fi set. Its curves and bluffs are meticulous but sit barren, like the face of a small, hot planet. We follow a shatter of Miller Lites into the main channel, between rubber tires and tangles of mesh that once stood in for the texture of marshes. The whole place is yellow and brown, "old gold," as my family says in Iowa. It's February, and the place is dry but sweet with the rot from water that collects in other seasons, and loud with birds the color of brambles calling out news of our arrival. Forty years after the Army Corps started digging, their model is still intact because precipitation can't ruin it and poison ivy moves too slow. When it rains here, water collects. After it was abandoned by engineers, the model moved on to a river's other purposes, to habitat and irrigation and the erosion of everything men put together. Above us, the silhouettes of sump pumps lean like rusty teakettles with switchboard lids, and the sky is netted with cold branches. On the drive we'd worried aloud for hours about getting lost, but as we hike further in the model directs us like a sunken path. All paths lead to the main channel. It's like walking along a fossil left by a centipede Godzilla would run from, but in the world of the river model it's us who are unfathomable. Here we walk like giant women up to our ankles in invisible currents. We keep our eyes down to skirt sharp islands and kick the trash aside.

no one had successfully escaped, but after sliding down the chute, Margaret Darcey fell 20 feet into the basement. She cut a screen, scaled the wall, and got away.

Denis Wood began finding lost underpants in shadowed spaces while living in Worcester, Massachusetts. He said the project started almost by chance, while he and a colleague were tracing the edges of rivers, circling lakes and ponds across the city. "In six weeks of casual encounter," he writes, "we came across a dozen pairs of pants, not looking for them, just tripping over them." Wood was teaching a class on water.

Chute is simultaneously the action of falling, as in "a quick descent or a river rapid," and a funnel, conduit, or physical shaft itself, the same way that a river is both water and a shape in the land where liquid has carved widely. The Roman aqueducts functioned entirely through gutters angled on a slight decline. Chutes were perhaps the first shapes that humans built to pull waste from their hands to somewhere else. Like a chute for laundry, a river is waste material and also waste space.

~

In Mississippi shipping culture "sounding calls" were the vocal signals a deckhand sang back to his pilot to announce the depth of the water approaching the bow. "Twain" is the measure of two fathoms, and "mark twain," the sounding call for 12 feet deep. Mark Twain, born Samuel Clemens, worked as a steamboat pilot on the Mississippi in his youth and later wrote about learning to read the river like a text: "There never was so wonderful a book written by man."

~

Scholar Ariella Azoulay argues that photography has featured many kinds of war but has left out any images of rape. Perhaps because the documentation of rape is more difficult to capture, more restricting than other suffering—where and when does it happen? In "Has Anyone Ever Seen a Photograph of a Rape?" Azoulay claims that because we lack examples in our archives and in cultural memory, the medium of photography has contributed to a widespread inability to recognize the reality of sexual violence as a strategy of war.

~

Meg is wearing Chacos with socks. She pries a brick from the floor of the model and tries to hand it to me without moving her feet. I wedge the soft rectangle into my backpack

~

"Garbology" was first coined in 1971 by A.J. Weberman, during a time when

between our two canteens, a bag of pretzels, and a mini mace. Ahead, the channel curls past the trees like an entrail. To my left, in the patchy sun, Meg's temple is shiny where her hair is streaked silver in the comic-book manner I've come to envy. "It's coming in hot this year," she'd warned me a week ago, over the phone. I've seen bleary pictures of Meg during college in long dresses and plastic beads. Shiny black hair, the same small, careful hands. Her grays first showed up when we shared a lint trap, a gravel yard, and a pair of brown flats back in Tucson, during the only years either of us have lived outside the watershed. Back then I slept in a square pink adobe facing the dry Rillito River and Meg shared the mother-in-law studio with our washing machine. Her house smelled like clean sweat, fabric softener, and the white smoke that filled her patio every morning. Two years and as many states later, she smells exactly the same way on a hike.

he was regularly sifting through Bob Dylan's trash. Weberman excavated the songwriter's street cans for years, looking for clues to the meaning of obscure lyrics. "All these years I've been looking for some kind of code sheet," said Weberman, known as the most unpleasant of Dylan's dogged fans. "I'm looking for a Rosetta stone to understand Dylan."

~

"How old is the Mississippi?" is a circular question because a river is both water and land. All rivers become rivers by extending their banks. The early Mississippi carried sediment that built this continent from bits of the places it had passed by, which is as good a metaphor as any I've heard for what America would someday aspire to.

~

~

Denis Wood writes that shadowed spaces also shelter acts that might be labeled "felonious."

Garbage, too, is contents and container. Calling something "the trash" defines non-trash areas by contrast. And shadowed spaces are those in-betweens where repulsive and attractive places meet for a tryst. So, every garbologist is, in fact, a curator, even if he imagines otherwise; even a digger with a strong stomach chooses something to discard, and that choosing is a story, though not often the story we imagine.

~

There are soggy underpants lining the rivers. Briefs, Wood says, at the banks. There are panties sold in bulk bags and on individual, transparent hangers. And there's a woman I love who wears smoke and detergent like a signature, whose life was divided at 19 when an acquaintance lifted her up on a washing machine, half-conscious, after a home football game, and left a dent where the back of her head met the cabinets.

~

The Mississippi flood of '27 drowned over a thousand people, but the exact numbers are unknown because the deaths of Black Americans were not counted in official records.

~

"It's almost magical sometimes," Wood writes, "how you can be, what? not two months older than your lover, but you're an adult and your lover's a minor and somehow THAT is no longer fooling around but a felony rap and a different life—not that anyone'd ever bring charges, except sometimes they do. . . ."

~

In February of 2001, A.J. Weberman was sentenced for money laundering; as part of the investigation, federal agents discovered evidence against him

Seeing us coming down the street, someone once called Meg and I "Christmas in the summer." Meg, a pear on legs, me a square piece of jerky. I didn't want to be Christmas, so I said, to Meg, "You do say 'honky-tonk' and mean it." "Yeah," Meg said, "and you eat ketchup with a spoon." Mornings in Tucson she would bang the screen door between the yard and my kitchen, where she'd heat coffee, steal milk and a mug, and tease whichever cat was feeling uptight. The deal was that Meg taught me about how weed cures a hangover, and I didn't tell about who came or went out the back gate in the dark. She liked men who worked with their hands and liked to say so. Meg hunted me down when I left t-shirts in the wash for so long that they dried together like a round, empty skin, and I taught her to use rubbing alcohol to pry cactus spines from her knees without breaking them. We made different messes. I knew Meg liked someone when she gave them a nickname that she could pronounce with an affected twang, but she only called me "baby" and then my first name. By afternoon she'd be on the edge of my bed with a hand on my back, saying "rise and shine." I'd moved with her into the pink house during the hottest part of that summer, out of a condo six blocks south, after a strange pair of underwear had shown up in my clean laundry. They'd gotten tangled in the bed sheets like something snagged by a current, and afterward my high school sweetheart moved in with his colleague and her baby across town. I threw away her pants.

by searching thorough his trash. "The garbologer was garbologized," said Weberman, "I was hoisted on my own petard."

In 1996, almost 20 years after writing "Shadowed Spaces: In Defense of Indefensible Space," Denis Wood plead guilty to "crimes against nature" and forcibly taking "indecent liberties with a minor" on "more than one-hundred occasions," after which he was sentenced to six years in prison.

A plaque at the Mark Twain Overlook in Muscatine, Iowa, thanks the writer for remembering Muscatine's sunsets. "The sunrises are also said to be exceedingly fine," Twain wrote, "I do not know." Twain is a local legend and a personal hero to my grandmother, who read *Life on the Mississippi* from her house on a river bluff marking the eastern edge of Iowa. My mother's first memory: the sound of a river barge's horn.

When my parents divorced, my sister and I left Brown's hill and moved to Iowa with my mother. This is how we grew up halfway on both sides of the river. We crossed the bridge on alternating weekends, belted into my mother's Jeep. The barges riding high and empty, or low and full of trash. Each passage a trade, a burden, a boundary. Each a new shade of homecoming.

~

In 1950, following the death of Georgia Tann, newspapers revealed that rampant abuse had taken place at the Tennessee Children's Home Society she headed. Among the grisly tales that surfaced was the frequent punishment of dangling children down the laundry chute from ropes tied to their wrists.

~

By now Meg and I have been walking a fake, dry river through the woods for an hour with no sign of an end. During the seven years the model was rushing with test floods, each shrunken city had its own upright sign, but in its current state I can't tell if we're in Memphis or Dubuque. Some of the tires are the size of a model city, and others have hosted small fires. Meg bends over the channel, tracing the billowing rim. The edge waves crazily to mimic bluffs and undulating drag—unique in every section of the model. It's shaped like the tunnel of an unstoppable wood borer. I realize this odd waveform might be the reason I came here in the first place. I confess this to Meg, who is trying to pry off a piece of it. "It looks like a language," she says, gritting her teeth. Meg's a poet, but it does. Like a signature from mouth to delta, or the

~

"There is a pornography of waste," writes Kevin Lynch, "just as there is a pornography of sex and of death. Slide-

delta waves of a long-sleeping brain. Everywhere we look the floor is carved with slender arcs and ribbons that scallop the bottom and sign the water's texture. Every scrawl, a note written from the engineers to the test waters, versions of shorthand for "riverbank."

~

As best I can remember, I've never thrown a piece of clothing into the trash that wasn't an undergarment, that wasn't stained or holey underwear or a bra of the kind Meg would describe as "dead," its underwire freed and stabbing at the secret place that is sometimes armpit and sometimes breast. Susan Griffin writes, "Whatever lies within the confines of the feminine province is defined sui generis as either trivial or obscene (as in housework, or lovemaking) and as such not fit for public discourse." Women's underwear serves as fetish this way because of its proximity and therefore likening to the body. Scholar Tracy Davis describes women's stockings similarly, as an early sexual garment that served as "the indexical sign of her skin."

~

Stuffed into nooks along side-yards, listing near worn footpaths and oily banks, the underwear I find is never the kind Wood has categorized. Neither thin hipped nor white, almost always made for those categorized as "women." Always cotton and a pattern not dainty enough for a child, nor

shows about Roman ruins usually include a few of the seats in Roman latrines. We are fascinated to see a building torn down. The abandoned houses in our inner cities are one of the most powerful images of the America metropolis."

~

Lynch, who died before Chernobyl, Exxon-Valdez, and Deepwater Horizon, advocated for the creation of "urban wildernesses," vital margins where children could find adventure and freedom from control. In the mid-'70s Lynch's *Wasting Away* imagined "waste cacotopias,"

so lacy as to be revoltingly called "panties" (when there are so many better words). They're the type of item that I once lost in college, drunk and outdoors in the middle of the night without a proximate or familiar indoor space to visit with the man who walked beside me. They were the same pair of underwear I discovered the next morning, soaking in a gray street gutter, where I recognized the garment for what it had become—trash—and abandoned it.

dystopic trash landscapes of the future: "The inhabited buildings slowly extrude their continuous ribbons of compressed garbage and trash. The ribbons fall onto the cargo belts that move steadily toward the high ridges at the city boundary. [. . .] Truant children play in these jungles too, and deplorable accidents are common."

~

In response to Azoulay's article, Canadian artist Zoe Leonard published a photograph of a stack of new, clean underwear ready to be handed out to patients at a rape clinic after theirs has been taken, forever, as evidence.

~

~

Before moving to Tucson, Meg was her hometown's favorite waitress during high school in rural Tennessee. She quickly learned about the ratio between lipstick and tips, and that summer her mother kicked her out of the house. The same August, along a different tributary, I started work on a cleaning crew for a leasing company in Iowa. The job taught me how to strip an oven without breathing Easy-Off, about which part of a rat decays first (eyes), how to clean a stubborn toilet ring with Windex and a toothbrush, and why the dustpan is the last item

Denis Wood's first guess was that the discarded underwear he found were the evidence of masturbatory acts hidden from the mothers who sort dirty clothes. "Fear of the laundry," Wood

in the rig you'd want to lick. My company was famous for cheating its party-school tenants and working-class staff, and during my second year it became popular for residents to shit in their showers just before moving out. We discovered two apartments where the tenants had been processing meth using the Jacuzzi tub in their master bath. The nicest place had pipe burns on the toilet seat, a freezer with three types of organic vegetables, and a medicine cabinet full of bras and underwear with their tags still intact. "No sticky fingers," said our crew leader, but by the end of the day he watched as each cleaner took her pick.

writes: "Fear of the wives and the mothers, the normative eyes with the normative hands that normatively do the wash, carefully screening each pair of pants for comely stains—Can anyone believe this of the laundress of a small hotel?" Wood asks, "Of a harried mother? [. . .] But such is the lens of paranoia our deviance presents our souls to use—and yet who knows? Perhaps there are such guardians of the norms."

~

Drawers. Intimates. Tap pants. Skivvies.

In the 17th century women's underclothes were "aired" rather than washed, and women often wore the same corsets for decades, until they rotted off.

~

~

Meg and I hear voices above us and we drop into the model on our elbows and knees. Someone is sitting with one boot outside a pickup on the slope. I mouth "trespassing," and Meg pulls off her red hoodie. We crawl around the bend, moving between panels of light that turn the bricks into

Wood later describes how shadowed spaces provide

gold foil as the voices disperse behind us. It's already late afternoon. The model here is cluttered with trash: Styrofoam and soda bottles and so many tires crowded together that I think they must be here for some game or agenda. Meg stands up, hands to knees and stage-whispers: "This is like the same shit from the real river, dried out." I nod, prying a splinter from my thumb. So much trash that no one would choose his pen name for a sight of the bottom. Because this part of Jackson is nearly suburban, the old river model has come to serve among its few out-of-site places.

~

A watershed is sometimes called a catchment. In city-planning terms the word *catchment* also describes the area served by one hospital, one fire department, one voting site, or one dump.

~

The dead end by our old house in Illinois was special in a second way because it was the place where I first met boys outside of school, three cousins who had found a perfect hideout by following their street uphill until it ended at a river view. They all wore rattails and had learned to run on their heels in shoes that were too big. They traded beads and a shiny hubcap for a perfect glass 40-ounce that I'd stripped of its label with dish soap and a sponge. This was the year when a friend told me sex was when a boy and a girl got into bed together and she let him pee in her underpants. It was the oldest one,

important refuge for behaviors that require safety, like early sex acts between young men. His point is not only that the places and the people a culture devalues often align, but that each tells something about the other.

~

"They see so well," writes Denis Wood, "they of the normative eyes: where can

the tallest cousin, who I let slip a hand up my shirt when he asked. We stood facing each other between the berry bushes long before my chest could warrant a bra. It was late fall and his fingers were so cold that I jumped. He laughed, and I did, and then we ran away in two directions.

we hide, we of deviant behavior?"

~

Underlace. Linen. Small clothes.

~

In *Hitman: Absolution*, a third-person video game released in 2012, players are assigned targets and complete levels once their target is killed. If successful, a player is invited to store the body of their victim in "body containers" throughout each level, including closets, manholes, outhouses, and laundry chutes.

There must be laundry chutes, or the material that once defined them, lying crumpled and stacked in dumps. Surely chutes also lie at the bottom of rivers below bricks and copper piping. Regarding trash and its destinations, one problem seems to be the idea of flushing—waste pulled from hands—that a river itself is both a direction and material for taking trash away.

~

Though the US Army Corps officially built the Mississippi River Basin Model, most able-bodied men at the time were fighting overseas. This meant that large sections of the model were designed and built by Italian or German prisoners of war, many of them handpicked engineers that Mayor Reybold transferred to a new internment camp near Jackson.

~

Meg came with me to Mississippi to see a place I couldn't fathom, no matter what we Google-imaged in advance. But with my feet in the state of Mississippi, I'm still surprised at the basic facts: that the Mississippi is the deepest part of a basin, that a watershed is antithetical to a river city, that the people who live there, the descendants of water, claim this very river for what they take out of it (street names, shipping, shellfish) but never what they put back (farm waste, tires, diluted shit). In the model I realize that I first learned the river ran down and that the cities it ran to were tinged with a type of afterward—places that accepted our runoff. Because in regional America, "downriver" is a type of extending margin, a relative shadowed space.

~

Short shirts. Knickers. Little Pants. Unders.

In 2006, the most radioactive object ever discovered by Scotland Yard was found at the base of a hotel laundry chute. The towel was eventually sent to a US nuclear waste facility, on consignment.

~

In 2009, the body of a 46-year-old Dominican-born cleaning woman was found, bound with duct tape, in the air duct of a Rector Street high-rise in upper Manhattan. Her case remains open.

~

Wood doesn't often address women or their deviances. But because women's work, done skillfully, remains invisible, and because the histories of many people are kept preserved by women, Wood must not have much to go by. And what from their archive is worth reviving? The best we've got are samples of tedious needlework, the well-preserved garments that others wore proudly. The best we have is unarchived. The best we have are the concentric depressions where stains were scrubbed from the tablecloth.

~

In 2010, a 24-year-old white Australian fell to her death 12 stories down a garbage chute with her jeans around her knees and a scrap of paper in her pocket with an unlabeled phone number. A podcast was made about her death.

~

What is obscene is often thought of as unwelcome because it has no proper audience and should be either hidden or eradicated. The materials specific to waste spaces have historically been deemed irrelevant based on their proximity to people who are also considered trivial, trash.

Today "white trash" refers to places like farm canals and junkyards. Places like hollers (which I used to imagine like a horizontal throat). Places like Iowa and Tennessee and Mississippi. The phrase also distinguishes itself from other slurs for people who live in thrown-away places. People differentiated from their white counterparts in that, in the minds of the speakers, they don't require a modifier.

Before the flood of '27, many free Black farm laborers migrated to the delta to become sharecroppers during the cotton boom. There, they were typically given the lowest lying acreage or

~

In 2015, a 26-year-old white legal secretary was found dead at the bottom of the D Casino's hotel laundry chute.

"bottomlands" along the river and contracts that forbade them from leaving during the crop cycle.

As soon as the flood hit, southerners began to think and talk about the water as northerners' water. Southern newspapers ran headlines like "Relieve the Flood Sufferers, but the Cure Lies at the Other End." The *Chattanooga Times* printed a comic entitled "The Thinker and the Problem," an image of Uncle Sam striking "the thinker" seated on the roof of a house and up to his knees in floodwater. What river landscapes show us is that violence, like trash, moves with gravity, from the powerful to the powerless, no matter what headlines say.

Authorities eventually ruled "no foul play," but never concluded how she fell 15 stories down the chute.

~

~

The tree line hinges open. Ahead, a metal walkway strides the river and extends to a rusty platform on the slope. Everything past the banks is caged in chain link, with us stuck inside a shape like an arena. Meg offers her knee. She pushes one hand against the bridge graffiti and the other against my butt. Later, I'll recognize this place in footage of the original flood tests. Here is the tower where engineers stood with clipboards and hardhats as their shadows dilated, watching to see what happened if they closed this set of levees or the other, measuring waterlines by centimeters.

"Hey!" Meg yells from below and moons me from under the bridge. Her butt looks exactly like the peach emoji I favor. I take her photo and she waits a minute before pulling up her tights. "Make it good, now," she says over her shoulder, glancing to either side. We haven't needed to say aloud that it's not the authorities we worry about running across out here. How free we are in a place with so many edges. A tiny

In 2016, a 58-year-old Black woman was found dead in the laundry chute in her home in Milwaukee, Wisconsin. Police considered her death suspicious, but eventually ruled it accidental.

~

landscape measured by careful hands, so far from polite spaces. Here is a place designed to be scrutinized. Now, as usual, we know we are what there is to see.

In 2018, an Irish man was acquitted of raping a 17-year-old after her underwear, "a thong with a lace front," which had been collected as evidence, was displayed for the court.

~

After Mississippi, I began asking women I knew about lost underwear. Where do they see it and where do they think it comes from? I asked relatives and students and mentors and friends. Trans women and white and Black girls and chicks from big cities and townships. Some were mothers, some had mothers, others not. One friend told me later that soon after we had met, I had given myself away as not-a-mother when I confessed that I did not know how to use bleach. Like these stories, the land that funnels water from Mississippi mouth to delta has never belonged to me, but the banks I've treaded do belong to them.

~

MISSISSIPPI

Wood: "Any space can be shadowed, if the time is right."

~

"What I register as women's underwear," "almost always designed for women," "overly female," "the decorative kind sold to girls," "what I recognize as 'women's' by color," "high femme," "hanging in trees along ski lifts," "in trees around a frat house," "I guess when I see women's underwear, I'm more inclined to think that they were left for bad reasons, and when I see men's or children's I think of an accident or maybe a prank," "I imagine the worst," "it's off-putting, I wonder about the potential violence. Or the potential pleasure, though it seems less likely to me," "there's something insidious about a woman's underwear on a street in this city," "in my mind the story is usually that there was some kind of late-night sex act that got disrupted, or sometimes it goes to thinking about prostitution and a woman fleeing to avoid the cops or to get out of a bad situation," "my reaction to them is fear and sadness. They represent some form of sexual violence," "always wet, as if washed up," "when I see underwear in public I get a flash of anxiety—certain that I'm witnessing the aftermath. I tend to tamp that flash as quickly as possible by imagining other possible stories: they fell out of someone's trash bag on the way to the alley," "there is also a very real feeling of being the witness to a crime," "I feel a small sadness, or maybe it's more like empathy. I think about the tenderness with which mothers treat their children. The proximity of motherhood," "I think of thrift store underwear, the challenge of keeping growing children clothed and the way my reaction to all bodily processes has shifted since I've had my own kids," "two years ago this would have really freaked me out (why would a little girl be without her underpants in a public park??) But now, as the busy hot-mess of a mom I've become, I just assumed that some parent dropped them while changing their kid into a swimsuit," "then, as I always do when I find unconventional trash in my environment, I wonder who it is in the world that picks it up and throws it away. Who will put everything back to normal? Not me."

~

Discarded underpants arrived just once at my dead end in Illinois. Sometimes at night, cars would park there with their engines off and their headlights pointed at the empty space above the river.

The pants I found one afternoon were made of shiny elastic and strangely thin on both sides. I had never seen a thong before. The only thing I thought to do was to bury them in the snow using the toe of my purple boot. After that they disappeared, maybe when my mother picked them up or the plow that piled drifts beside the house came to scoop the mess away.

~

Wastewater and women have historically done the cleaning up, though primarily women of color have done the cleaning up for white women. Not always in the same ways as water does, not always with the same waste. But the bodies of cleaners, like their places, often enough end up downriver.

~

Now there is my own underwear tied up in someone's sheets. An old pair lost to the drain. Smalls. Pretties. Scanties. All the hands allowed to press themselves against our lining. And underwear, a sign of the skin and what's below it. Places where women read in their waste that time is cyclical and not a straight descent. Like how sometimes you'll find older, more brilliant leaves dying slowly against the wet of the ground beneath hundreds gone brown and crisp above them.

The observation tower above the Mississippi River Basin Model has four levels laced with sagging metal stairs that form a double Z. Meg stays below to photograph the graffiti. In the distance stands the enormous water tower I see lurking at the back of the old operational footage. I notice how thoroughly the undergrowth has clotted the model and how, from up here, I can't make out anything behind us or ahead. Brown bottles and green glass litter the corners of the platform, stuck with wet leaves. On my way back down, a pair of stained underpants, yellow or yellowed by rust, dangle above the river from a railing like some kind of flag. Then a single sneaker. A graying Ace Bandage. Evening is soaking up the short end of the sky. Meg helps me down again and we raise our hoods and agree to turn back in 20 minutes.

~

In Muscatine, Iowa, my grandmother is helping to spearhead the reintroduction of Higgins eye mussels, once native to the Mississippi. River mussels filter moving water. And in spring my grandmother will watch as divers wade into the dark waters and drop new Higgins shells along the riverbed, each tagged with a black dot of glue. Together the new mussels will work like a tiny sieve, cleaning not the water that comes to the city, but water the residents won't see again. The new mussels filter the water that the city sends downstream.

~

As a kid I'd believed the rumor that a girl could get pregnant from swallowing semen—in one end and out the other. The body—by now, you must admit—is an original kind of sieve, a chute, a foul channel. And the end of that canal is integral, its relationship to gravity the reason for the garments some of us turn over at common boundaries. The word they teach us is discharge, but some women I know say they believed something was going wrong with them downriver for the first few years. That dense, quotidian material, sign of health and fecundity, and the colors of panties—red and black, pink and cream.

~

Shreddies. Drains. Unmentionables. The organ-like smell of the places where dead leaves touch.

~

At the end is the delta. Small cleats stand up evenly from the riverbed like points mapping a grid. No sump pumps. The river model dilates until it's all ruffled edge and knotted tributary and nowhere smooth to walk. It looks like the cracked patio of some failed regime, and in the center sits a sun-bleached folding chair. Meg holds out both arms and spins; here we're the right size again. It's taken us two hours to walk from the spot where she rolled me in over the fence and our canteens are empty. Meg laughs as I pull my tights below my knees and squat over a shallow ribbon that a careful hand carved into this model before our mothers were born. She takes my picture. The current leaves me and divides into several channels, the way it will across the delta.

A KNOT,

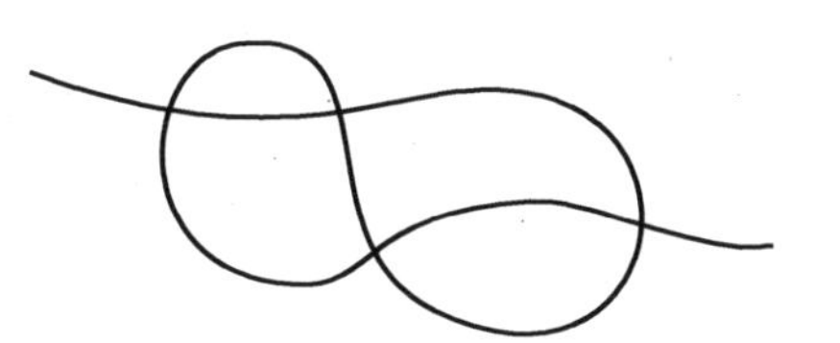

A LEAN

I lost my final baby tooth in the way-back of a passenger van while chewing on a cotton drawstring. I had never pressed my face into a pair of red basketball shorts before, and though I did have something going for the kid who the shorts contained, I was honest-to-god just helping him out before the sharp turn arrived. I confessed precisely all of this to my mother on the loud shoulder of the highway, bleeding softly from the mouth. Knots come easily to cotton drawstrings, I told her, and are best loosened with front teeth. This is known, I said, as my incisor lay against the wheel well. I was eight and compelled by a guilt I couldn't name. I have a thing for knots.

—

#363 is the code for "The Vampire Suitor," according to the Aarne-Thompson-Uther system, a tool that folklorists use to categorize stories across time. Some of the regular plots have worn threadbare on television (#410: "The Sleeping Beauty"), but many more are forgotten (#1212: "The Horse Is Drawn Across the Ice"). The ATU system maps basic trends using 2,500 numerical codes to label plots from the Hans Christian Anderson tales to new Hulu series. It's a system of categories that claims to reveal a collective unconsciousness among us, a narrative redundancy we can't seem to escape.

—

He began by sending me short porn clips as pretense, as one theoretic body exploring another. We had been dating for two months, kissing prostrate until our mouths swelled. "Do you like that?" he'd ask, hitting send on a cobalt hyperlink. "ya," I'd type, "that last part," in 10pt Georgia, hot pink. Though essentially I was afraid or in awe, sometimes stirred, otherwise studying what gravity did to folded skin in arrangements I hadn't yet imagined.

—

Elsewhere: "My underwear is different." Just that thought, removed from reason. Scrunched. And the tie on my pants . . . not tied the way I tie it. A metallic smell like the spray from a garden hose and that look on the face above mine.

—

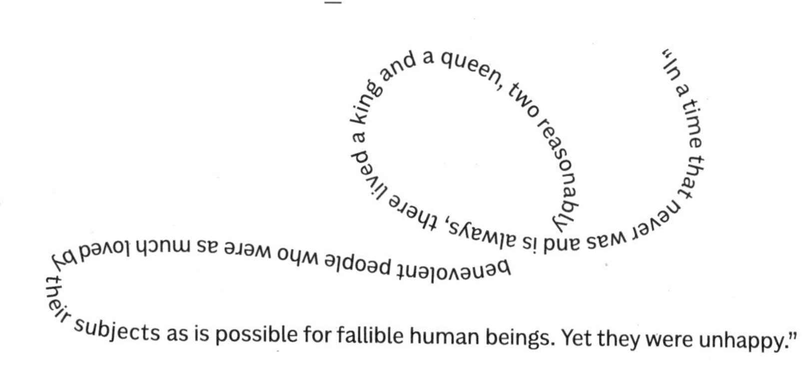

—

The preface to a 1987 popular reference volume, *The Folkloresque*, begins with a story that "everyone knows": A visitor to an asylum observes the inmates alternately calling out numbers to one another. In response to the numbers, the gathered group erupts in varying degrees of laughter. The visitor's host explains that, for reasons of economy, the residents there have assigned a number to every known joke. The visitor tries out this scheme by calling out a figure of his own. "41!" he yells, and is met with silence. "Some can tell a joke," his host explains, "and some can't."

—

Before I got to dance as a kid, I was gifted *An Illustrated History of Ballet* so I'd be sure about what I was getting my parents into. In my family, we begin at the library. The book didn't say much about keeping time or about mirror-walls or the way pubescent nipples blink and shimmy through a leotard. Instead it contained adaptations of old stories. Long sections about set design and orchestral music and the choreography of a narrative.

—

Thompson suggested that the Aarne-Thompson system could be named "The Types of the Folk-Tales of Europe, West Asia, and the Lands Settled by these Peoples." Later it became the Aarne-Thompson-Uther system to remedy that by expansion. The ATU labels a story by its most recognizable motif, and then by submotifs—those echoed in more distant narratives. For code #410, there are at least 76 individual related myths. In this manner, the system lays out a web in which each recurrent story is linked to similar and then less similar tales.

But the ATU is not a universal map. The idea that humans tell only a specific set of tales suggests a deeply held nostalgia for the story. The idea hints at a string of narrative genotypes, the grip of learned tropes that we can never escape, the way engrained hatred and patriarchy are said to reproduce themselves. I too need short units of meaning. I wish to inhabit a small violence that once happened to me. One I still can't reconcile.

—

My thing for knots started when my mother let me tie up her hair. I was still very small, but I remember thinking about how beautiful she was going to look afterward, as if her hair was full of great looping braids. I remember how she cried when we pulled at them hard, first with a hairbrush and then with a comb, and then, eventually, we had to cut them out.

—

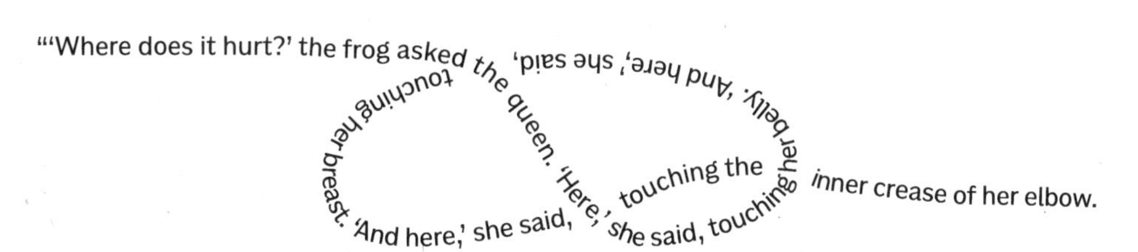

'I ache for what I lack.'"

—

There's this image I've started seeing everywhere. I recognize it even in silhouette. It's two bodies—nothing in the fore or background. The first body is prostrate and the second body leans in toward the first. It's the enchanted woman and the hero. It's Dracula and his hot lunch. It's *The Gross Clinic*. It's a perfume ad for Dior. You'll start seeing it now, too. It's the doubled gaze, the precipice, the plot turn, or the moment just before a death. Yesterday it was Google's home screen.

Like the tales in our limited set, *the lean*, as I've come to think of it, is an archetype, but of a new brand. It's the image of the void lengthening impossibly before the climax. It lets us linger as long as we like, and I can't stop looking. There is something there that I am trying to remember. Something I want, or have been instructed to want, like being chosen, or taken, or brought to life by a man. Perhaps it's the long lean itself—that acceleration. That sailing forever toward a hero's deed. An impossible reach I want to frame and feel in my marrow. In scenes of the sleeping woman where she is pictured alone—the VHS cover of *Snow White*, *Rosemary's Baby*—I know that I am employed in the lean.

What we know is that everything that comes after this image is boring. Everything is midlife. Resolution. All death or marriage as we know it. We have arrived at a peak.

—

I was in the back of a passenger van, gnawing diligently at the shorts of a bewildered family friend who had tied his waistband too tight, when my mom took a hard left turn. My incisor came out in the way it might have if it were tied to a string tied to a doorknob and then slammed—with immediate vacancy and without pain. Except that the tooth hadn't been ready to come out, so I bled slowly through our tissue supply.

—

Most of us can now recognize the exact shame of shuttering a browser dispatching porn. Like others born in the era of the home computer, I watched bodies engage in ordinary sex acts onscreen before I attempted them myself. The watching transpired first and in highest frequency soon after I started up the kind of teenage relationship so overwrought that it gets revisited in frantic outbursts for the next long decade. He was far from being a man, but it was he who introduced me.

—

If my family has a religion, then it is the practice of American medicine. The trappings of the two institutions are so alike that to map them is to map them in excess. The subtext is that promise of fending off death—the exchange of immediate and long-term salvations. The houses of worship are full of symbols (often the same), innumerable doorways, floor-length uniforms, white light. Further on, in unadvertised rooms, the working class clatters and sweeps and questions their devotion. Babies go through the front doors, bodies go through the back.

—

An Illustrated History of Ballet taught me that in the Tchaikovsky version of "La belle au bois dormant" (#410 The Sleeping Beauty), a group of 12 old, knitting women are killed for leaving their spindles close to the kid princess. I also learned that in "Perceforest," the oldest entire version of the story, as in many others, the prince impregnates the comatose woman he discovers and leaves without waking her.

—

Not yet a teen and at the summer camp I would later get kicked out of for "kissing," I was discovered alone in my bunk, hiding out from the swimming period like I had been since I first felt the muck at the bottom of the lake. There, tied to my bedpost, were perhaps 40 friendship bracelets, the kind with tedious chevron knot patterns. The longest one was belt-length. The head counselor who found me scolded at first but stopped herself short. Then for a long time she looked from my face to the bracelets and back again, like she was deciding whether or not it was time to consult the nurse.

—

Myths haunt us. Are we fated to reenact their patterns like the victims of systematic trauma who reproduce their own violence? Or perhaps we are doomed because each story houses some core machinery that motivates us to retell. Maybe some stories are wired to infect and use us like a virus, to propagate among us unseen.

—

He sent the videos and I received them. Our generation's adolescent social scene was among the first to launch itself on the Internet. We were a community under rigid curfew with a vibrant nightlife in LCD. Much has been said about the risk of anonymous virtual space and transactions that arise in the absence of a face, a voice, and a human-sized reaction time. But back then we recognized these dangers and went on deftly perpetuating them across a distance that afforded us the type of exchange so taboo to previous generations who had looked many more people in the eye.

"O red the blood and white the bed. A spindle dart will pierce her heart. And then not fall to death but sleep. Silent, still and fathoms deep."

—

The first thing out from an egg looks up from its nest. As up from a well. Some blinking. I find myself coming-to a lot. Because I pass out pretty often. I don't like to call it fainting for reasons you might guess. In the moment before consciousness, I always get stuck in a tunnel. A cartoon peephole. Nothing gauzy or unhinged. Just the sky and a barrel neck. It's the same under sedation. It's the same every time. Like a bullet snug in its chamber. It smells like the rubbing alcohol that is out past the light, but I'm stuck and staring at the slow channel. It was in there, once, that I knew something was wrong.

—

In the older versions of the story, the sleeping beauty wakes because after being visited, she has delivered a baby in her sleep. Modern scholars read the girl's sleep as a dormant period between childhood and puberty and the waking a wakening into womanhood. In some versions, the belle bears twins who suck the poison from her finger, seeking a nipple with rosebud lips. In one of the oldest known stories, the girl wakes up and notices a child in her room. "Oh," she says, "A man has been here!" I can't help but laugh aloud.

—

Pornography trades in tropes shaped by specific media. Like all genres, there are patterns you can't recognize unless you've spent some time with each of its forms—print, poster, video cassette, JPEG, MP4, GIF.

Most of the famous porn archetypes are left over from early films only available on video and international cable—the pizza girl, the bad babysitter, the nurse. Those born on the internet are easily recognizable because most could exist nowhere else. Online, the pretense and storyline is reduced to match the speed of a click, but one can see how some premises remain because they contain something particularly illicit that the anonymous Internet perpetuates. This is what made archetypes like the first ones, and also why they deserve a kind of undoing.

—

Before I was born and long before AIM, his father and my stepdad smoked cigarettes together by the back doors where the bodies were carried out. We grew up visiting hospitals because they were places of work. Our fathers wore white or pastel clothing with small bits of steel attached. They wore rubber soles in cold hallways threading complex doors. My birth father was out our door before breakfast and not home until after bedtime until he left my mother for my stepmother, his nurse. Later, my stepdad walked heavy and sometimes sat quietly in his office after work because he performed surgeries on dying children.

My own fathers were both working men who slept little and poorly. I got used to their calloused hands. Neither was particularly father-like, except while bedside, but they made things possible for many people, and also for me.

—

In the four years following that van ride, my teeth crowded in around the resulting gap impacting the late bloomer buried above. By the time I sat down in my first orthodontics recliner my upper centerline had moved three teeth to the left and two teeth behind the gap where the eyetooth had been torn away. By the end of my visit, the doctor informed my mother that the tangled arrangement had impacted the new tooth so severely that it would require a surgical procedure and sedation to get it out.

—

"'Is it not strange,' said the philosophers of the south, 'that so much should be built upon so little?' And the old women who herded the sheep spinning the fleecy thread as they went, clapped their hands to their lips, 'What will become of us now?' they cried."

—

Most of the pictures in *An Illustrated History of Ballet* featured famous costumes and set designs. On one page was *The Death of Sardanapalus*, an 1844 painting by Eugène Delacroix depicting the rape and slaughter of the women among Sardanapalus's possessions he ordered to be destroyed after learning of a military defeat and then immolating himself. Stage designers had taken inspiration from the work's vivid brush strokes and red hues, but I cracked the spine of my book just there because I returned often to see the woman in the painting's lower right corner. She is dying, or about to start. A man wearing a turban bends her backward as he buries a dagger in her breast from behind. He is *exotic*, is someone far away. She is naked, candescent, even as a drape or a dress falls from her hand, but she does not look entirely pained or sad. His weapon is mostly hidden behind her, and without it he could be gently pulling her toward him, or hero-like catching her in a fall. She is what we are supposed to look at amidst the chaos of a massacre. She is something on the brink.

—

as a fish is drawn by an angler's line."

—

Many years and many medical intake questionnaires later, I finally explained to a physician that very likely a dental surgeon had once handled my unconscious body in an unauthorized manner. In a manner that forever afterward made me balk at a sterile swab. I looked straight at the doctor while she asked if I was sure and if I knew exactly what I was implying. Then I let my features lay flat in the expression of a person who is listening as the doctor explained that clothing can move around during any operation. "The whole body loses muscle control," she said, "And with gravity in the mix, you're kind of slowly sinking in the chair. Everything can ride up, get loose and open." Then I began to feel sick.

—

"Drat!," the original Sleeping Beauty says to the camera in my mind's eye, "I've multiplied!" Now she's talking above the laugh track. "Where is the scoundrel who thinks he's getting away with this?" before she seeks that man out and takes him as her husband—an old reversal of that agency. So perhaps that's the real tune in this background. The chick that picks in the shell. The act of secret rape pivots a tale requiring the Beauty to seek instead of being sought after. Maybe then the story is a medium for normalizing that violence. The story hopes that we learn to read without concern, or, better yet, to commiserate, to see within that sleep-rape an inherited joke.

—

There is something sacred about noticing a person's chest hair fill in over a small window of time, and also something obscene. Pretty soon, we were rehearsing choreography that I had thought crude and uncomfortable on screen. Those same motions that became meaningful with practice. Shortly before that we had gotten bored online, and the stream of videos he was sending had taken a different tone. I was less shocked, or he was posturing, and so instead the experiment became a demonstration in variety. A shift from the instructional to the cautionary. The spectrum became less titillating and more unknown. Shortly after that I first saw sleeping porn. That was what he liked.

—

Artist and critic Elizabeth Brown-Guillory has written that, through the Eurocentric gaze, the exoticizing of Asian culture is also "a means of containing the threat of its power." In many sleep videos, the camera is set on a bedside table so the whole thing looks homemade. Very often, the "sleeper" is an Asian woman, a trope having to do with racial stereotypes perpetuated in porn which depict Asian women as passive or innocent. The men are white. The women stretch and make small sounds as if they are dreaming during the whole event. They are actors, playing at unconsciousness.

—

—

What was clearest to me about *An Illustrated History of Ballet* was that *The Death of Sardanapalus* was visually erotic and probably forbidden to me. I returned to images then as I do now, in secret, as a hidden practice, to stare at what is so often a violence well masked as sex. I could always claim that my initial pull toward that image was the tug one feels in the face of a master composition. That it was Delacroix's coaxing of light all along. But if I'm honest it was the tension that both repels and draws me to the suspenseful narrative—the void that stretches before a body whole but held up against a violence.

It's Andromeda tied before the monster, King Kong approaching a well-roped blonde. It's somewhere in *Jaws* and *Jurassic Park* and the hunting of every beauty. It's not the composition of the lean, but it's that same action. The slow-sail, the buzzing that diminishes, the passive body impossibly stilled and the active body approaching. A tension that could inspire in anyone a proclivity for binding and for being bound.

—

"And there would have been two people present at all times," said my doctor. "It's a policy, in surgery," she emphasized and then looked up. "Do you remember if the nurse was male too?"

—

It is difficult to describe the vulnerable female body without displaying it erotically. I have only been under anesthesia twice. Just a pair of tonsils and the impacted eyetooth. I was 15 and on my back and lit from above. I was in a dentist's chair. The eye of my elbow was host to cold fluid, and I was wearing sweatpants with a tie. First they had to cut in through my gums to fish it out. There was a lot of blood. Next they attached a bracket to the face of the excavated incisor. They hooked the bracket to a chain. They cinched the chain tight to a tooth in the knot below. They stitched the gum together. Then there was some time left before I came to. Everything that happened to my body during the surgery and after it happened with hands. Everything. Very little was mechanical.

—

About recurring myth, Travers says: "Perhaps we were born knowing the tales from our grandmothers and all their ancestral kin run through our blood repeating them endlessly, and the shock we give when we first bear them is not a shock of surprise but of recognition. Things long unknowingly known have suddenly been remembered. Later, like streams, they run underground."

—

Before Disney there was the German "Dornröschen"; the Italian "Sole, Luna, e Talia"; the Irish "Queen of Tubber Tintye"; "The Petrified Mansion" from *Bengal Fairy Tales*; Cymbeline; King Peacock; Endymion; "Chundun Rajah"; "Little Surya Bai"; "The Accursed Garden"; "The Water of Life." But even the newest stories suggest the sleeping girl is raped—she is sleeping until birth or until the child she births wakes her. The process is decidedly carnal.

—

Whenever *the lean* ghosts an image, even one without humans, that image will be compulsively reproduced. The paintings entitled *A Horse and a Lion* (1763), *Horse Frightened by Lion* (1763, 1770), *A Lion Attacking a Horse* (1770, 1772), *Horse Attacked by Lion* (1769), and *A Lion Devouring a Horse* (1763, 1823) are all versions of the same hunting scene, likely first depicted in a carving that stands in the Palazzo Dei Conservatori, later mimicked by the romantic painters Théodore Géricault and George Stubbs, whose obsessions with the scene spanned 50 years and more than 20 images. Examples of *Lion and Horse* paintings break the hunt and consumption of the horse into stages.

Basil Taylor writes that the first iteration of the scene shows "the frightened horse in a rocky landscape, the lion being missing." In 1763, immediately after viewing Stubbs's painting of *The Startled Horse*, Horace Walpole wrote: "How pois'd betwixt the love of life and dread,/ With yielding joints, with wild distended head. . . ."

Taylor calls the second iteration (which recalls Sardanapalus), "the most favoured composition." In these paintings the lion clings to the white horse's back, mouthing its spine as the horse torques its head sharply, candescent; the lion takes its first bite and the horse still cannot see him. So many versions of this image exist that some call it the final scene.

But Théodore Géricault began his *Lion and Horse* series after Stubbs. He had vowed to revive portraiture from its steady decline through dynamic scenes like *The Raft of the Medusa* and by imbuing animals with human traits. There are fewer versions of Géricault's later depictions of the Lion and Horse and the scene in his lithograph entitled *A Lion Devouring A Horse* is yet uncategorized by Taylor, but I'll call it *D: The Kiss*—The pure equine is prostrate. The hunt is over. The lion bends to eat.

—

Some of the videos look like they are shot at a party. Some are so amateur that you can hear the other people in the room, as in the famous, unwatchable scene from *Rules of Attraction*. The staging suggests that a girl has just passed out. These are the ones that seem made to suggest a kind of validity. These claim a kind of truth that propagates.

It has been about a decade since I saw the worst video and I can't bring myself to search for it again. Back then it was the one I believed was real—the violation of an unconscious woman. He thought the validity would be interesting to debate. Even now I inch awake when the clip appears at the back of a dream.

—

I have waited this long to tell and the truth I know still seems inexplicable. In the meantime, I have told myself many other things.

—

Some scholars still think of #410 as the original nature story, a personification of the earth awakening in spring after a long winter, out of a prolonged chrysalis, the way Persephone rises after biding her time. What is unique about this group of stories is the motif of false death, the prolonged absence in sleep. Long before them there was Brunhilde and Perceforest and all the oral stories that brought the sleep tale our way.

—

Some harm is known only in the body. Even these decades later, my tooth remembers its years in my head, and it recedes slowly, tilting, returning to a familiar root.

—

"'There are more ways than one of entering a room,' said a soft, alluring voice. 'Perhaps,' a musical laugh rang out, 'I came in through the key hole. Come now and see what I am spinning.'"

—

The *Illustrated History of Ballet* featured Sardanapalus because the painting was an inspiration for Michel Fokine's set and choreography for "Scheherazade," a section of the ballet *One Thousand and One Nights*. Scheherazade told the story of a Persian king who discovered his wife had been unfaithful to him. He killed her and resolved to marry a new virgin each day and to behead the previous day's wife so none could ever betray him. The king had killed 1,000 wives by the time Scheherazade asked to spend the night with him. She was a bookish woman, versed in myth and in history and in poetry. Once she arrived in the king's chambers, Scheherazade began telling stories to her sister, a chain of stories so riveting that they persuaded the king to keep her alive for another night. After 1,000 stories and nights, the king fell in love with Scheherazade, and by knowing the old stories well enough she had saved her own life, and likely her sister's, too.

—

Sleeping Beauty is a 2011 Australian film, in which the protagonist, Sara, is a young college student who gets paid to take heavy sedatives and "sleep" beside men who have agreed to "no penetration." We tried watching it together, he and I, though I was wary. In the first minute of the trailer, a kind of madam tells Sara, "Your vagina will be a temple." The madam ensures Sara that the teas she drinks to sleep will make her even more beautiful. I started retching when she first lays down.

—

Even now I am not reliable to myself. The operation worked. Nothing resulted but a specific repulsion. I need and need to look away. Most stories, it seems to me now, are about looking or choosing not to.

—

"Outside, among the tents, the storytellers' heads were nodding; Acrobats slept in mid-somersault. The camels turned to stone."

—

I admit that I played the sleeper when he asked. We did just what we had seen on screen. I lay immobile as long as I could.

—

Most people must know someone still walking the earth, with whom they first tried out everything. I mean everything sexual they both could think of at the time. That kind of practice is a kind of love itself, a sort of reverence. A hard knot to untie.

—

In *Sleeping Beauty*, a performance-art installation at the National Art Museum of Ukraine, Taras Polataiko enlisted women to lie sleeping for two hours each day from August to September of 2012. Visitors to the exhibit who wished to participate were required to sign a contract stipulating that they would marry the woman if she opened her eyes to their kiss. One volunteer told the press, "If it's my true love, I will feel it on an intuitive level." The premise is that the sleeper decides to wake if the kiss is the right kind. The nuance is important. A joke if the sleeper chooses wrong.

—

One afternoon, in the depths of my university library, I called the elevator with some tact, my arms full of fat pornography references with their spines turned in toward my own. One especially useful volume declared itself "PORN 101" in a large noble font. You may be less surprised than I was to find that there is limited information about porn away from the Internet. But there was something about heavy print that seemed a decided way to begin.

—

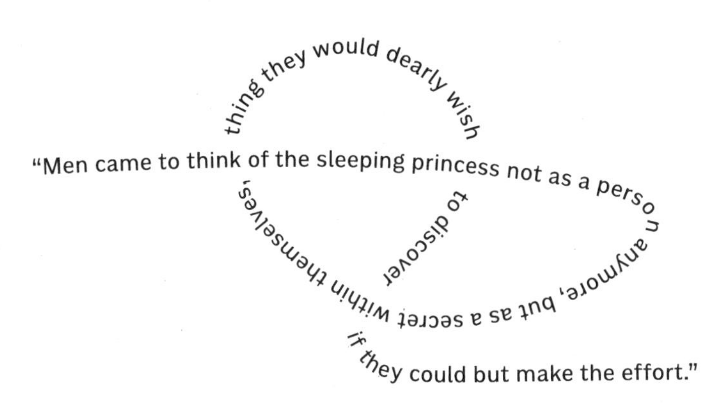

—

There is information a doctor knows but can't say in words. A surgery is a passage across bodies. A transaction. A permissive violation. A giving over of control. At some point, microscopic bits of the surgeon's body and the patient's will combine.

—

A professorial type greeted me when the library's elevator arrived. "Whoa, little lady!" he exclaimed, pressing his arm against the door sleeve as if to widen it as I reined up on some proverbial steed of internal transport. To be plain, I was wearing pigtails, but I had meant them as ironic.

"Are you *reading* all of those?" asked the man, who I could see was gripping an important notebook. "I'm not sure yet," I admitted. "Just doing some research," glancing between him and the hot digits enumerating themselves. "Research," he nodded, sagely, "What are you studying?"

I sighed audibly and swiveled toward him. "Can I just show you?" I pleaded, letting my hardbacks tumble to the sticky carpet. We smiled together as he pulled a length of comfortable rope from his back pocket and I jammed the emergency stop and, reader, is this the subtext of all such interactions? Is there a tired heteronormative elevator-porn-premise cuing every quotidian encounter? If so, I think that might explain what I feel I'm missing sometimes—the shorthand vernacular to categorize a pressing nuance. That heavy wink at the bottom of things.

—

Sleeping porn is the medium, but not the root. It reveals the winnowed grain. Sometimes pornography inspires specific acts, but most of the time "the situation" has no impact at all. Not every watcher reiterates the acts they see, or behaves under porn's influence.

—

The point of most jokes is to reveal an uncomfortable or obvious truth. And the truth about college libraries is that patrons do not frequently transport whole stacks of the books they contain.

Sometimes things do happen, of course. Situations one can't control or didn't plan for, but become exciting. Situations that make a person unsure how to position their body in one moment with a stranger, and for some time afterward without them. But on most occasions, one simply dismounts the elevator and makes for the circulation desk where a luckless student has to unearth the barcode branded to each heavy porn textbook.

—

One doesn't have to read all of "The White Album" to know that "We tell stories in order to live," is not something Joan Didion meant literally. One only needs to read the line that follows directly after. The second line of the essay: "The princess is caged in the consulate."

Somehow, through repetition out of context, there is often a literal invocation of Didion's line that feels related to the lean. I seem to encounter it everywhere. It's the same sentiment that avoids discomfort around immobility in a narrative. And it is the attitude that drives some of us to forget that a paragraph which begins "We tell ourselves stories in order to live" ends with "We live entirely, especially if we are writers, by the imposition of a narrative line upon disparate images, by the 'ideas' with which we have learned to freeze the shifting phantasmagoria which is our actual experience." The same attitude that insists on the cliché of evoking a myth in the first place, of inspecting a fairytale too closely.

—

Out of the five women who agreed to sleep and be kissed in Polataiko's exhibit, only one opened her eyes, and it was in response to the kiss of another woman. This complicated the contracts significantly, because gay marriage is still illegal in Ukraine.

"The two women appeared surprised by the entire incident," said the press, who treated the whole thing as a silly mishap—a trick played on the sleeper herself that reversed a certain gendered outcome Polataiko's exhibit seemed to expect.

In an official statement, the Byzantine Catholic Patriarchate in Ukraine stated afterward that the woman-to-woman kiss moment in "Sleeping Beauty" was "not just an innocent play, but actually an ideological means to promote perversion."

"I had no idea that my quiet and innocent piece would end up causing such turmoil," said the artist Polataiko.

—

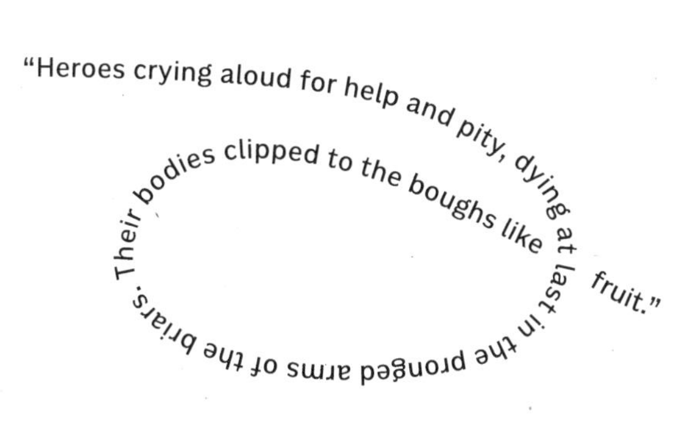

—

In eastern traditions, Mary is spinning a bloodred thread when the Holy Ghost enters her through her ear in the form of a dove, and she conceives Christ. In college, I once attended a lecture on the few Annunciation paintings in which Mary is depicted as surprised, or afraid, rather than serene.

—

The operating room was very small and without windows. I had been unconscious and reclined for over an hour, sedated. Does that word bother everyone?

Soon, I looked out from inside myself at the span of distance receding. Like a long tube but also like a rumble strip slowing the process. A tug—a warning that goes unseen. Something wrong. An expression on the doctor's face that would be difficult to distinguish from any doctor watching any patient wake from any anesthesia. His eyes waiting to meet mine. Pain far from my teeth.

After that, I remember the knots—I ran my tongue across them. They were jagged and Plasticine and high beneath my cheek so that if I curled the lip it would stay lifted there above the stitches until I pried the skin away. What remained was a restraint.

Our family knew everyone at the hospital, of course. My fathers taught them or played tennis with them or shared their lunch break and knew all their kids. That doctor moved away. Sometimes I imagine him out there, operating. That my not-telling, my living on, will have perpetuated his long lean.

—

The reason for telling a story is not the distance it affords the listener, the looker-on. Nor is retelling for the pleasure of being closely tied, bound up with that person. Retelling is unbinding, providing the occasion for a listener's future release.

—

Five days after Polataiko's performance closed in Ukraine, a similar mythic performance opened at Fashion Week 2012. In *Sleeping with Gaga*, pop star Lady Gaga wore a black dress and "slept" for an hour on a black bed inside a giant empty bottle of her fragrance, "Fame." She was inaccessible to visitors. The performance was live-streamed, and its feed mostly displayed Gaga and her attendees, who were invited to spritz themselves with samples beside the artist, encased in glass.

—

One reading suggests that in isolated sleep, in an era when female performing artists were taking over their industry and posing questions about their own commodity, Gaga took control over an ancient storyline. Instead of "marrying herself off," *Sleeping with Gaga* seemed to insist that a visitor might only lean in for a while before paying the lady for her wares. For some piece of her that they might otherwise have been allowed to physically take away.

—

The original Aarne-Thompson list does not classify "Scheherazade"—it's a story once considered "outside" the Western canon, and perhaps kept there because of its power. In missing this very old tale, perhaps the reverse of the lean, the A-T system discounted, among other things, the narrative act of avoiding climax and resolution, and instead choosing the kind of structure that keeps everyone awake.

—

"Face to face with the Sleeping Beauty—who has long been the dream of every man," Travers writes, "and the hope of every woman—we find ourselves compelled to ask: what is it in us that at a certain moment suddenly falls asleep?" Except that is decidedly not the question. The viewer is not the horse nor the sleeper—I have no questions for her. I want to speak to the leaner-in. I need to know why he went to so much trouble. How many others slept after he stood beside me.

—

"He knew himself to be at the center of the world and that, in him, all men stood there, gazing at their heart's desire—or perhaps their innermost selves. He trembled, aghast at his own daring."

"'He is himself his own weapon,' said the woodcutter, 'The time must be ripe.'"

—

It's not the childhood that sleeps—not the aging process, nor the season, but our protagonist that is put on hold. Her sleeping produces a partial cut, a frame that forces our story to be defined by lack. A story about the old desire to serve up a body made silent.

—

In porn we find all our modern retellings. Our sleeping girl is still well framed. The rising action is brief. She invites us to lean and to interpret. She may be faking it. No one else will see.

—

If we classified it, we might start to think of "Scheherazade" as the categorical opposite of #410. It's the story of a victim turned trickster who avoids sleep and silence. The story's conclusion is not a culmination, but a reversal. Silence hovers around all but the central character—the woman the story is named for, who has a real name. It's a story about looking, and telling. Scheherazade makes use of that impulse. Only then can she undo a repeated violence in order for every character to live.

—

"'I have been dreaming about you,' she said simply. For indeed, what else had been her preoccupation all these sleeping years?"

SIGNAL, ARIZONA

Yes a peach pit has a name for the brown hollow of your elbow. It's the same name the coyotes use—boasting against sirens—for the wild alleys sunken through the city where we live. Last night I saw a javelina barrel past the art museum like she was after something good. The light turned red for her. Seems like I've never breathed that hard—and why?

One-two-one-two the homing sound out at the boundaries again. Rangers drink up at the dry trailheads without the loam of decaying roots. *Make cactus arms* they say to the new ones before the first gut punch. The middle school where I work has a glass daycare so the girls there can make small hands at their babies during gym. In August I work in the park. Capture bees in soapsud Dixie cups. I take the best bodies for myself after the count. Pat their drowned wings at my sink. A Mason, a Leafcutter, Carpenter, a Cuckoo. My ranger says our killer swarm escaped a local lab. *Persistent pollinators so we can't catch them*. They'll hover over water to wait for you. You run a mile if they're after you and you don't fall down. Listen—who colonizes a desert? Bones fell asunder and were mingled with others here. What is intended by our nothing grief? You say a bow is only alive when it kills but the purpose of this city is unfounded. Some-one has been tagging saguaros at my catch site. Proclaiming makeshift love in silver paint on the tallest. It had grown four arms—one for each century. My ranger told me that, the both of them green. Now it festers.

That nothing will outlive us is no reason for subsisting. Not that or the nothing heat. And the architectures of my smallclothes? Heaped and silvered in the corners of your cabin? I leave my husks here so you can never forget that or what you owe me. Please quit this silence. I prefer that from now on, we only converse in shapes. Please place the shape of your idea here:

ACKNOWLEDGMENTS

Thank you to Caryl Pagel for her intuition, her writing, and her keen eyes, and everyone at Rescue Press, Danny Khalastchi, Alyssa Perry, and especially to Annie Leue and Sevy Perez for bringing these visual forms to life.

Thank you to the magazines and journals that first published versions of these essays: *Conjunctions* (Winter 2013), *Black Warrior Review* (Fall 2014), *Hotel America* (Fall 2016), *The Normal School* (Fall 2016), *Territory* (Spring 2016), *The Atlantic* (October 2018), *Mid-American Review* (Spring 2017), *Diagram* (18.2), and *Ninth Letter* (October 2018). Particular thanks to editors Nick Greer, Lisa Ampleman, Steven Church, and Philip Graham. "Log Cabin Square" appears in *Best American Experimental Writing 2020* and in *Advanced Creative Nonfiction: A Writer's Guide and Anthology*. "Into the Limen: Where an Old Squirrel Goes to Die" appears in *Welcome to the Neighborhood: An Anthology of American Coexistence*.

This writing was supported by grants from the Vermont Studio Center, the Hambidge Center for the Arts, and the American Scandinavian Foundation. Research for this project was conducted at the Musser Public Library and at the National Pearl Button Museum, both in Muscatine, Iowa, at the State Historical Society of Iowa in Iowa City, at the Cedar Rock House (Frank Lloyd Wright) in Quasqueton, Iowa, at the Mississippi River Basin Waterways Experiment Station near Clinton, Mississippi, at the University of Arizona Main Library, the University of Arizona Poetry Center and in Saguaro National Park West, all in Tucson, Arizona, at the Alden Memorial Library in Athens, Ohio, and at the Kelvin Smith Library at Case Western Reserve in Cleveland, Ohio.

Special thanks to Karen Zimmerman and Phil Zimmerman of the University of Arizona Visual Arts Department, to Miriam Intrator and Michele Jennings of Ohio University Special Collections, to Courtney Kessel of Ohio University Galleries, to Derek Faust of the Doppler Project, and to Geneva Murray of the Women's Center, who were each integral in supporting the adventures this book has had in three-dimensional forms.

Diane LeBlanc was my first writing teacher. I am indebted to Kaethe Schwehn, who introduced me to experimental essay forms. Kate Bernheimer led me back to the old stories and then back to myself. I am grateful to Susan Briante for encouraging my strangeness and to Alison Deming for the study of plants. There will never be enough thanks for Ander Monson and I will be grateful eternally for his experimental pedagogies, his example of lifelong learning, and his very many very brief emails. Most of this writing is finally here because of Eric LeMay's tireless support, generous spirit, and digital adventures—thank you endlessly. Thank you also to my neighbor, Dinty W. Moore, for Kenyon, for friendship, and for my favorite garden. Thank you to the writers who taught me how to teach, Laynie Browne and Renee Angle.

Thanks to Meg Wade, Sarah Rose Nordgren, Nina Boutsikaris, Piper Daugharty, Susanna Hempstead, Christine Adams, Elizabeth Tran, Derek Robbins, Zoë Bossiere, Maggie Messitt, Megan Kimble, Cory Aaland, Gretchen Henderson, Daisy Pitkin, Noam Dorr, Andrea Francis, Lawrence Lenhart, Jim Huber, and many more, for your support, and your insights.

Thank you to my mother, Meg, the moon.
Thanks to Andrew Dietz, a fellow writer.
Thank you to Sarah and Roger Lande and to Grace and Bob Minor.

Thank you, Thomas Mira y Lopez, for all semicolons, and for a life of love and writing. These objects would not be here without you.

This book is written in dedication to my sister, Liza.

SELECTED WORKS CITED

Arnold, Joseph L. *The Evolution of the 1936 Flood Control Act*. Fort Belvoir, Virginia: U.S. Army Corps of Engineers, 1988.

Ashliman, D. L. *A Guide to Folktales in the English Language: Based on the Aarne-Thompson Classification System*. Vol. 11 of *Bibliographies and Indexes in World Literature*. Westport, Connecticut: Greenwood Press, 1987.

Bachelard, Gaston. *The Poetics of Space*. Translated by Maria Jolas. New York: Penguin Classics, 2014.

Bahn, Paul G. *Cave Art: A Guide to the Decorated Ice Age Caves of Europe*. London: Frances Lincoln, 2007.

Benyus, Janine M. *Biomimicry: Innovation Inspired by Nature*. New York: Harper Perennial, 2009.

Brown-Guillory, Elizabeth. "'Feet Don't Fail Me Now': Place and Displacement in Black Women's Plays from the United States, South Africa, and England." *College Language Association Journal* 57, no. 2 (December 2013): 95–110.

Carter, Angela. *The Bloody Chamber*. London: Vintage, 2006.

Chapman, William, dir. *Lascaux, Cradle of Man's Art*. Chicago: International Film Bureau, 1950.

Cheramie, Kristi. "The Scale of Nature: Modeling the Mississippi River." *Places Journal*, March 2011. https://doi.org/10.22269/110321.

Crane, Eva. "Wall Hives and Wall Beekeeping." *Bee World* 79, no. 1 (1998): 11–22.

Damanhur Inside Out. damanhurinsideout.wordpress.com/.

Federation of Damanhur. The Temples of Humankind. https://www.thetemples.org/.

Elias, James, Veronica Elias Diehl, Vern L. Bullough, Gwen Brewer, Jeffrey J. Douglas, and Will Jarvis, eds. *Porn 101: Eroticism, Pornography, and the First Amendment*. Amherst, NY: Prometheus Books, 1999.

Ettema, Robert, and Cornelia Mutel. "Hans Albert Einstein: Innovation and Compromise in Formulating Sediment Transport by Rivers." *Journal of Hydraulic Engineering* 130, no. 6 (June 2004): 477–487.

Foster, J. E. "History and Description of the Mississippi Basin Model." *Mississippi Basin Model Report 1-6*. Vicksburg, MS: U.S. Army Engineer Waterways Experiment Station, 1971.

Griffin, Susan. "Red Shoes." In *The Next American Essay*, edited by John D'Agata, 311–316. Saint Paul, MN: Graywolf Press, 2003.

Landman, Neil H. *Pearls: A Natural History*. New York: H.N. Abrams in association with the American Museum of Natural History and the Field Museum, 2001.

Mellor, Emily, and Simon Duff. "The Use of Pornography and the Relationship Between Pornography Exposure and Sexual Offending in Males: A Systematic Review." *Aggression and Violent Behavior* 46 (May–June 2019): 116–126.

McPhee, John. *The Control of Nature*. New York: Farrar, Straus and Giroux, 1989.

Pajaczkowska, Claire. "On Stuff and Nonsense: The Complexity of Cloth." *Textile: The Journal of Cloth and Culture* 3, no. 3 (2005): 220–249.

Pokrefke, Thomas J., and John J. Franco. *Investigation of Proposed Dike Systems on the Mississippi River: Hydraulic Model Investigation*. Vicksburg, MS: U.S. Army Engineer Waterways Experiment Station, 1981.

Rahn, Herman, and Tetsuro Yokoyama, eds. *Physiology of Breath-Hold Diving and the Ama of Japan*. Washington, DC: National Academy of Sciences National Research Council, 1965.

Romero, Aldemaro, Susanna Chilbert, and M.G Eisenhart. "Cubagua's Pearl-Oyster Beds: The First Depletion of a Natural Resource Caused by Europeans in the American Continent." *Journal of Political Ecology* 6, no. 1 (1999): 57–78.

Stevenson, Ian. *Reincarnation and Biology: A Contribution to the Etiology of Birthmarks and Birth Defects*. Westport, CT: Praeger Publishers, 1997.

Taralon, Jean. *The Grotto of Lascaux*. Paris: Caisse Nationale Des Monuments Historiques, Service Commercial, 1962.

Travers, P. L., and Charles Keeping. *About the Sleeping Beauty*. New York: McGraw-Hill, 1975.

Uther, Hans-Jörg. *The Types of International Folktales: A Classification and Bibliography, Based on the System of Antti Aarne and Stith Thompson*. Helsinki: Suomalainen Tiedeakatemia, Academia Scientiarum Fennica, 2004.

Windels, Fernand, and Annette Laming-Emperaire. *The Lascaux Cave Paintings*. New York: Viking, 1950.

Witzling, Mara. "Quilt Language: Towards a Poetics of Quilting." *Women's History Review* 18, no. 4 (2009): 619–637.

Wood, Denis. "Shadowed Spaces: In Defense of Indefensible Space." Scotland: Arika, 2007. http://home.arika.org.uk/archive/items/shadowed-spaces.